READ TO WORK

AGRICULTURE

SUSAN ECHAORE-YOON

CAMBRIDGE ADULT EDUCATION
A Division of Simon & Schuster
Upper Saddle River, New Jersey

Author: **Susan Echaore-Yoon**

Series Editorial Consultant: Harriet Diamond, *President, Diamond Associates, Multifaceted Training and Development, Westfield NJ*

Reviewers:
Margaret Kirkpatrick, *Berkeley Adult School, Berkeley CA*
Jackie Anger, *Institute for Labor Studies & Research, Cranston RI*

Director, Editorial & Marketing, Adult Education: Diane Galen
Market Manager: Will Jarred
Assistant Market Manager: Donna Frasco
Editorial Development: Learning Unlimited, Inc.
Project Editors: Douglas Falk, Elena Petron
Editorial Assistant: Kathleen Kennedy
Production Director: Kurt Scherwatzky
Production Editor: John Roberts
Art Direction: Pat Smythe, Kenny Beck
Cover Art: Jim Finlayson
Interior Design & Electronic Page Production: Levavi & Levavi
Photo Research: Jenifer Hixson

Photo Credits: p. 6: Jose Carillo, Stock Boston; p. 14: Larry Lefever, Grant Heilman; p. 22: Matthew McVay, Stock Boston; p. 32: Michael Newman, Photo Edit; p. 40: Kathy Sloane, Photo Researchers; p. 48: Scott Aldrich; p. 58: Lefever/Grushow, Grant Heilman; p. 66: Michael Dwyer, Stock Boston; p. 74: Janice Fullman, The Picture Cube; p. 84: Robert Brenner, Photo Edit; p. 92: (Mark E. Gibson; p. 100: Stephen R. Swinburne, Stock Boston.

Printed in the United States of America
2 3 4 5 6 7 8 9 10   01 00 99 98

ISBN: 0-8359-4682-7

CAMBRIDGE ADULT EDUCATION
A Division of Simon & Schuster
Upper Saddle River, New Jersey

CONTENTS

TO THE LEARNER

Welcome to the *Read To Work* series. The books in this series were written with you, the adult learner, in mind. Good reading skills are important in the world of work for these reasons:

- They may help you get the job you want.
- They will help you learn how to do your job well.
- They can help you get a better job.

The lessons in this book, *Read to Work: Agriculture,* will help you improve your reading skills. As you work through the lessons, you will also learn about jobs in farming, horticulture, animal care, and gardening.

UNITS

Read To Work: Agriculture is divided into four units. Each unit covers different kinds of jobs. You can look at the **Contents** to see what fields and jobs are covered in this book.

LESSONS

Each unit contains at least 3 lessons. Each lesson teaches one reading skill and covers one kind of job. Here are some things to look for as you read each lesson:

Words to Know are words you will learn in the lessons. Look for the meaning of each new word to the left of what you are reading. You will also see a respelling of the words like this: *pronunciation* (proh-nun-see-AY-shun). This respelling will help you say the word correctly. There is a guide to help you with the respellings on page 105.

Job Focus describes the job in the lesson. It also tells you what types of skills are needed to do the job.

How It Works teaches you about the reading skill and how you can use it.

Readings include memos, pages from handbooks and manuals, posters, product guidelines, safety notices, and articles from company newsletters. If you look through this book, you will see that the reading passages look different from the rest of the lesson. They are examples of reading materials from the world of work.

Check Your Understanding questions can be multiple choice, short answer, or true/false. They will help you check that you understand the reading.

On the Job gives you a chance to read about real people as they do their jobs.

OTHER LEARNING AIDS

There are other learning aids at the back of the book. They are:

Resources: where to get more information on the jobs in the book
Respelling Guide: help with pronouncing words
Glossary: definitions of the Words to Know
Index: job names in the book
Answer Key: answers to *Check Your Understanding* and *Lesson Wrap-Up* questions

Now you are ready to begin using *Read to Work: Agriculture*. We hope that you will enjoy this book and learn from it.

· Jobs in ·
Produce Farming

Produce farming is one of many kinds of farming in the agriculture industry. Produce farmers need workers to plant seeds, remove weeds, pick produce, and do other basic jobs. They need workers to watch over work teams and help run the farm. Farmers also need workers to sell their produce to the public.

In this unit, you will learn about some materials that produce farm workers read. They might read notes and letters from their bosses. Often these materials describe how to do jobs safely. Also, produce farm workers might read books, magazines, and other materials. The information that they learn can help them improve their job skills.

This unit teaches the following reading skills:

- finding a main idea that is stated in the reading
- finding details that support the main idea
- finding a main idea that is not stated

You will learn how workers in produce farms use these reading skills in their work.

Working Safely in Farming

▼▼▼▼▼▼▼▼▼▼▼▼

Words to Know

employees

Human Resources

manual

memorandum (or memo)

precautions

supervisor

Suppose you work on a produce (PROH-doos) farm. On this farm you grow fruits and vegetables. You get this job note:

> To: All Workers
>   For safety purposes, a new rule has been made. Please follow the new safety rule as of today. It is: When driving any farm machine, wear the proper clothing. You must wear a hard hat, gloves, and steel-toed shoes.

The job note talks about safety. It is an example of the kind of material that you might read on any job.

In this lesson, you'll read some materials about working safely on a farm. Farms have safety rules to keep workers from getting hurt. Workers must follow them carefully.

When you read work material, you need to know what the point is. In other words, you must **find the main idea.** In this lesson, you will learn how to find a main idea when you read.

Job Focus

Farm workers plant seeds and seedlings, remove weeds, and pick produce such as fruits and vegetables. They plow fields, mix bug-killer sprays, and water plants. Farm workers also drive farm machines and repair equipment.

Farms usually hire large numbers of farm workers only during certain parts of the year, such as at harvest time. However, many farms have a crew of full-time workers throughout the year. Farm workers who have many farm skills and strong basic skills have better chances of getting work.

Finding the Stated Main Idea: How It Works

The **main idea** is the most important idea in a reading. Often, writers state the main idea. You can usually find the stated main idea in the opening paragraphs.

For example, let's look at the **memorandum,** or **memo,** on this page. The main idea of the memo is stated in the first paragraph. Read the first paragraph. Then, underline the sentence that you think states the main idea of the memo.

memorandum
(mehm-uh-RAN-duhm) a short note or reminder; memo is short for memorandum

employees (ehm-PLOI-eez) people who are hired to do work for a company or business

---

M E M O

Date: April 24
To: All Garcia Family Farm **Employees**
From: Al Garcia, President
Subject: CONGRATULATIONS, SAFE WORKERS!

I am proud to report that in the last 365 days, we have had <u>no</u> injuries. Nor have we had any accidents. All employees at Garcia Family Farm are indeed safe and successful workers!

This is a great record. It shows that you all take pride in your work. You work carefully and safely alone and as a team.

To honor your safe work habits, the Farm will hold a special lunch. Please come to a barbecue on Friday, May 8, from 12:00 noon to 2:00 p.m. The place--the front lawn.

Keep up the good work! Let's have another safe year.

The main idea is *all employees at Garcia Family Farm are indeed safe and successful workers!* Everything else in the memo supports this main idea.

Read the rest of the memo. The second paragraph talks about how the employees work. The third paragraph talks about a special lunch for the employees. The last paragraph tells the employees to keep working safely.

Read the third paragraph in the memo. Underline the main idea of that paragraph. The main idea of the third paragraph is *to honor your safe work habits, the Farm will hold a special lunch.* The other sentences in that paragraph support that main idea.

arm employees might read a memo like the one on this page. It is about a safety problem. Read the memorandum. Notice that the memo has the words *To* and *From* near the top. The *To* line tells who gets the memo. The *From* line tells who wrote the memo.

Human Resources
(ree-sawrs-uhs) the department in a company that keeps all employee records, such as records of sick leave

precautions
(prih-KAW-shuhnz) actions to prevent danger

supervisor
(SOO-puhr-veyez-uhr) someone in charge of other workers

MEMORANDUM

Date: January 5
To: All Employees
From: **Human Resources**
Subject: Safe Rules--Using Ladders

Over the past six months, several employees have had accidents while on ladders. Please be careful! It is easy to lose your balance.

We want to remind all employees of the following safety rules. Please take these **precautions** each and every time you use a ladder.

Rule 1: Carefully check a ladder before using it. Make sure that it is free of dirt, mud, and oil. Check that all of its parts--the rails, rungs, and braces--are fastened. If you find a ladder that is not safe, report it right away to your **supervisor**.

Rule 2: Set up a ladder carefully, on firm and even ground. Make sure all the feet touch the ground. Make sure the braces that connect the rails are locked. If the braces are not locked, the ladder could tip over.

Rule 3: Test the ladder before climbing. Step on the first rung. Place your full weight on the rung. If it feels wobbly, get off immediately. Talk to your supervisor about the problem.

Rule 4: Climb safely. Hold the rails of the ladder as you climb. Always face the rungs of the ladder. You should never climb above the third rung from the top.

Rule 5: Work safely. You should always feel balanced on a ladder. When standing on a rung, keep both feet on it at all times. When reaching to pick fruit or to cut branches, reach only as far as your arms can go. Do not lean any farther.

Answer each question based on the memo on page 4.

1. The main idea of the memo is stated. What is it?

   a. Over the past six months, several employees have had accidents while on ladders. (first paragraph)
   b. Please take these precautions each and every time you use a ladder. (second paragraph)
   c. Work safely. (seventh paragraph)

2. The main idea of Rule 1 is stated. Which sentence states the main idea?

   a. Carefully check a ladder before using it.
   b. Make sure that it is free of dirt, mud, and oil.
   c. Check that all of its parts—the rails, rungs, and braces—are fastened.
   d. If you find a ladder that is not safe, report it right away to your supervisor.

3. The main idea of Rule 2 is stated. Which sentence states the main idea?

   a. Set up a ladder carefully, on firm and even ground.
   b. Make sure all the feet touch the ground.
   c. Make sure the braces that connect the rails are locked.
   d. If the braces aren't locked, the ladder could tip over.

4. The main idea of Rule 4 is stated. Which sentence states the main idea?

   a. Climb safely.
   b. Hold the rails of the ladder as you climb.
   c. Always face the rungs of the ladder.
   d. You should never climb above the third rung from the top.

5. The main idea of Rule 3 is *test the ladder before climbing*. That means

   a. employees should check for damage to the ladder.
   b. employees need to fix the ladder before they climb it.
   c. employees must make sure the ladder is steady enough to hold their weight.
   d. employees should see if the ladder has already been used.

Check your answers on page 113.

Martin is a farm worker. He is a full-time employee for a large produce farm. One day he hopes to have his own farm. Martin's supervisor thinks Martin is one of the very best workers. So he asked Martin to teach other employees to do new tasks.

One day Martin taught Angel, another employee, how to mix a bug-killer spray. First, Martin told Angel to read the safety rules for handling materials used for mixing bug-killer.

Then Martin said, "Now, I'll show you the special clothes we have to wear." They went to the closet to get the clothing. Martin took out coveralls, face masks, goggles, and gloves. Each man put on a pair of coveralls. Then Martin gave Angel written instructions about how to wear a face mask.

"The mask should cover your mouth and nose," said Martin. "You don't want to breathe any bug-killer. You can get sick."

Martin led Angel to the room where bug-killer materials are stored and mixed. He explained the safety signs on the walls.

Martin pointed to other signs by the shelves. He said, "These are the instructions for the different bug-killer sprays. Before you mix one, always find its instructions. Read the instructions over."

"All right," said Angel.

"Always read the instructions," Martin repeated, "even if you know how to mix the materials. It's easy to forget a step."

Angel nodded.

"Read these instructions," said Martin. He pointed to a yellow sign. "I'll go get the materials we need."

TALK ABOUT IT

1. Describe two things that Martin and Angel read when they are working with bug-killer materials.

2. Explain why reading is an important skill for Martin and Angel.

manual (MAHN-yoo-uhl) a book of instructions for employees

Many companies give each worker an employee **manual.** These manuals have information that employees must know about their work and the company.

Most manuals have a section on job safety. Here is a page that farm workers might read in a manual. Read the safety precautions. Then, answer the questions on the following page.

SAFETY PRECAUTIONS—LIFTING OBJECTS

Lifting objects as light as one pound or as heavy as 50 pounds can be done safely. Follow the safety precautions when you lift objects. They can help you prevent a back injury.

1. Use your head.

Before lifting an object, plan how you'll lift it. Check out the object. Think about how much it weighs. Can you handle that weight? Think about its size. Will it be easy for you to handle?

Test how heavy the object is. Pick it up a little way to make sure you can lift it. Lift it higher only if it feels O.K.

2. Use the right muscles.

Using the right muscles to lift things can prevent a back injury. Many people think those are the back muscles. They are not! The correct lifting muscles are your leg muscles. The leg muscles are more powerful than the back muscles.

3. Lift objects properly.

Plant both of your feet firmly on the ground. Stand so your feet are shoulder-width apart. Your toes should point out. Before you lift, bend at your knees. Tighten your stomach muscles. That will support your spine when you lift. *Do not twist your body as you lift an object.*

4. Hold objects properly.

Hold the object that you're lifting close to your body. The closer an object is to your body, the less pressure is put on your back. And keep your back straight at all times. By doing this, you are only carrying the weight of the object.

5. Ask for help.

If an object is too heavy or too large, do *not* try to lift it! Get help when you know an object may be too hard to lift alone. Ask one or two co-workers to help you. Arrange for a hand truck, forklift, or other help. If you have any problems, talk to your supervisor.

Job Safety   19

FINDING THE STATED MAIN IDEA   7

Find the main ideas of the safety precautions on page 7. Write the sentences that are the main ideas. Explain why they are main ideas.

Example

The main idea of **1. Use your head** is *before lifting an object, plan how you'll lift it.*

This is the main idea because *the other sentences describe what things to think about and plan.*

1. The main idea of the whole reading selection is

This is the main idea because

2. The main idea of **2. Use the right muscles** is

This is the main idea because

3. The main idea of **3. Lift objects properly** is

This is the main idea because

4. The main idea of **5. Ask for help** is

This is the main idea because

Check your answers on page 113.

◆ LESSON WRAP-UP

In this lesson, you've learned about some jobs that farm workers on produce farms do. You've read safety materials that they might read on their jobs. You've seen how important it is to understand the main idea of reading materials.

You learned in this lesson how to find a main idea that is stated in a reading. Every reading has a main idea. That is the most important idea about a subject. If a writer states the main idea, it will be found in the opening paragraphs.

You also learned that every paragraph in a reading has a main idea. Sometimes, the main idea of a paragraph is stated. The other sentences in that paragraph support that main idea.

At times, workers get reading materials that are hard to understand. If you can understand the main idea, it will be easier to understand what you read.

1. Think about other materials that you have read. You may have read them at home, at work, or in school. How can finding the main idea help improve your reading?

Finish the sentence below.

Finding the main idea will help improve my reading because

2. Think about materials that you have read on the job. The job may be one that you have now. Or it may be a job you have had in the past. What did you read? Why was it important to understand the main idea of what you read on the job?

Write a paragraph based on the questions above.

Check your answers on page 113.

Selling at a Farmers' Market

<table>
<tr><td>

▼▼▼▼▼▼▼▼▼▼▼

Words to Know

association

bountiful

customers

display

efficient

haggle

quality

</td></tr>
</table>

You might see a sign like this in a shop window in your town.

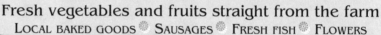

WOOD SQUARE FARMERS' MARKET
Wood Square Shopping Center
Every Thursday, 9 A.M. to 2 P.M.
Fresh vegetables and fruits straight from the farm
LOCAL BAKED GOODS ✿ SAUSAGES ✿ FRESH FISH ✿ FLOWERS

A farmers' market is a place where owners of small farms can sell their produce. Other kinds of local sellers come there too, like bakers and fishermen.

The farmers and their employees read rules and permits for selling at the market. They also read material about selling produce. In this lesson, you'll be reading some of these materials.

In the last lesson, you learned how important it is to find the main idea of a reading. **Finding details that support the main idea** can also help you understand what you read. In this lesson, you'll learn how to find these supporting details.

Job Focus

A farm employee who sells at a market may do some of the following tasks: deliver produce to market; set up and break down the booth; sell produce; and be in charge of permits, forms, and other paperwork.

Farmers' market workers are salespeople. They should have good speaking, reading, writing, and math skills.

Many farmers sell their produce at several farmers' markets throughout the week. And new farmers' markets are opening up in many cities.

Finding Supporting Details: How It Works

Every main idea needs **supporting details.** The details tell more about the main idea. They explain things about a main idea, such as *what* or *who, when* or *where,* or *how* or *why.*

To figure out how a detail supports a main idea, ask yourself, "How does the detail explain something about the main idea? Does it support the main idea?"

For example, the reading below gives sales information for farmers and their employees. The main idea of the piece is stated. It is the sentence in *italics.*

How to Set Prices at the Farmers' Market

customers

(KUHS-tuh-muhrz) people who buy things from a store or business

Your produce can be the best around, but **customers** won't buy if they think prices are too high. *Here are some tips to help you set prices.*

1. Find out how much local supermarkets are charging for their produce. Try to keep your prices the same or lower than theirs.
2. Set prices so that making change is easy. Use amounts such as $0.75, $1.00, and $1.50.
3. Post signs that list your prices. Many customers like to see prices before checking out the products. And posting your prices may mean fewer customers will try to **haggle** with you.

haggle (HAG-uhl) to bargain or argue over prices

4. Lower your prices when needed. Are customers complaining about your high prices? Are customers reading your price signs and not stopping? Then, think about lowering prices to make more sales.

The main idea has four supporting details. What do you think they are? The main idea is *Here are some tips to help you set prices.* Therefore, the four supporting details must be tips for setting prices. The details that support the main idea are:

- *learning the prices of produce at local supermarkets*
- *setting prices that are easy, round numbers*
- *putting up price signs*
- *making prices lower to get people to buy your produce*

Did you notice that each supporting detail was given in a new paragraph? Each supporting detail is explained in a way that tells you more about the main idea of the reading. All the parts of the reading work together to give you complete information. You learn about the main idea, and you learn about each supporting detail.

association
(uh-soh-see-AY-shuhn) a group of people or businesses that share some interests

Farmers' markets are usually run by an **association**. The association prints information sheets for farmers who sell at the markets. On this page is an example of an information sheet for farmers and their employees. Read the information sheet.

How to Sell Your Produce— And More of It!

At a farmers' market, you must be a salesperson. Be one that customers remember, so that they come back to you. Here's how you can become that kind of salesperson.

❋ Customers like friendly service. Sometimes all it takes for someone to stop at your booth is a friendly "Hi! How are you?" Always have a smile ready.

❋ Customers like polite service. "Please." "Excuse me." "May I help you?" "Thank you." Customers know when these words are said sincerely.

❋ Does your service show pride in your produce? Customers like that, too. Let customers touch and feel your fruits and vegetables. Also, slice up some of your produce and give samples to your customers to taste.

❋ Does your service show enthusiasm about your produce? If you have a chance, talk to your customers about how you grow things. You might give tips for storing fresh produce. Or you might suggest ways to prepare and cook the produce.

❋ Last, customers like **efficient** service. Arrange your booth so that you can serve customers quickly and easily. Have your bags ready. And have enough small change handy. Always serve one customer at a time.

By the way, wear your overalls. They, too, can help you sell more of your produce. Wearing overalls tells customers they're buying produce from a real farmer. And that's what you are!

efficient (ih-FIHSH-uhnt) doing something well with the least amount of time and work

---

Answer each question based on the information sheet on page 12.

1. The main idea is stated in the reading selection. It is *be a salesperson that customers remember so that they come back.* In your own words, explain what this means.

2. Five important details support the main idea. Choose those five details from the following list.

   a. Salespeople should always wear neat, clean clothes.
   b. Customers don't like to eat free samples of fruit and vegetables.
   c. Being friendly helps bring customers to a booth.
   d. Customers can make their own change.
   e. Customers like a polite and sincere salesperson.
   f. Salespeople should show that they like the things they're selling.
   g. Customers like to buy products when they know the salesperson takes pride in them.
   h. Customers like a salesperson who is always talking.
   i. Salespeople need to serve customers easily and quickly.

3. Suppose you work at a farmers' market. You sell apples and pears. Give examples of the ways to give good service. The first one is done for you.

   a. Enthusiasm about the fruits: I would give customers a recipe for making apple pie.

   b. Friendliness:

   c. Politeness:

   d. Pride in the fruits:

   e. Efficient service:

Check your answers on page 113.

My name is Sherrie. I work for a farmer, Mrs. Lee. But I don't work on her farm at all. I work for her in the city where I live. I sell her produce at the farmers' market. I've been doing this job for over a year, and I've learned a lot about farming and selling.

Mrs. Lee's farm is more than 150 miles away. She grows vegetables—like garlic, tomatoes, corn, potatoes, and sugar peas. She also grows Asian vegetables, like bittermelon and bok choy. Her workers deliver the produce to the farmers' market. I meet them there an hour before the market opens.

First, I read a note from Mrs. Lee. It tells me what vegetables I'm selling and how much to charge for them. It also tells me anything about the produce that may help me sell it. Then I read the recipes that Mrs. Lee types up for me to give away.

I always go through a folder to read the forms that we must have on hand. I make sure everything is there. I post our permits.

When that's done, I do my favorite task. I make the table look pretty so that customers will stop and buy our produce. I arrange the different vegetables so they look nice next to each other.

When my first customers come by, I can usually count on someone saying, "What fresh-looking vegetables!"

"We grow only the best!" I tell them with a smile.

TALK ABOUT IT

1. Describe two kinds of materials that Sherrie reads on her job.

2. Is reading important for Sherrie to do her job well? Why or why not?

Many farmers and their employees read farm magazines for helpful information. Sometimes, the magazines have stories about selling at farmers' markets. The magazine article on this page is an example. Read the article. Then, answer the questions on the next page.

Farmers' Market Notes

MAKE AN EYE-CATCHING DISPLAY

Imagine that you're standing in front of two booths. In one booth, the produce lies in a dirty mess. In the other booth, the produce is clean and put into neat piles. Which booth do you think customers will go to?

That's easy. Customers will go to the booth with neat and clean produce.

Farmers, you may have **quality** products—the best at the farmers' market. But nobody will know it if you don't know how to show it. To draw customers to your booth, make a neat, eye-catching **display.** Here are some ideas you might try.

◆ **Make a display that's neat and clean!**

Clean your produce before you put it out. Wash or wipe off dust and mud. (Would you buy a dirty piece of fruit?) Remove any produce that is damaged or spoiled.

◆ **Make a display that's colorful!**

Take advantage of the colors of your produce. Mix greens, reds, yellows, whites, and so on. The colors of your produce will appeal to customers. They'll stop to see what you have.

◆ **Make a display that's easy to see, easy to touch!**

You want customers to see what you have. They can't see produce lying flat in the boxes. Prop up boxes and slant them toward the customer. Put your produce at an elbow-to-eye level. This lets customers see the produce. And, yes, touch the produce, too.

◆ **Make a bountiful display!**

Make it look like you have a lot of produce. Customers are more likely to shop at a booth that has a big selection. So keep your display well filled throughout the day. If you have only a small amount of produce, you can still make it seem like a lot. How? Space out the vegetables on your tables.

One more thing: After you've set up your display, stand in front of it. Imagine you are the customer. Would you stop? (The answer should be "Yes!")

---

quality (KWAHL-ih-tee) how good something is

display (dih-SPLAY) a showing or presentation of items

bountiful (BOUN-tuh-fuhl) a lot

Answer each question based on the article on page 15.

1. Go back to the reading selection. Underline the main idea of the article. Then, write the main idea below, using your own words.

The main idea is

2. The main idea has four supporting details. Find those supporting details. What are they? Explain why they support the main idea. The first one is done for you.

   a. One supporting detail is "*make a display that's neat and clean!*"

   It supports the main idea because *it tells one way to make an eye-catching display.*

   b. One supporting detail is

   It supports the main idea because

   c. One supporting detail is

   It supports the main idea because

   d. One supporting detail is

   It supports the main idea because

Check your answers on page 113.

◆ LESSON WRAP-UP

In this lesson, you learned about farm employees who sell produce at farmers' markets. You read materials that workers might read to help them sell their products. You found out how important it is to understand the supporting details in a reading.

You've learned in this lesson how to find supporting details for a main idea. Details support or explain something about a main idea.

Often, workers read materials that help them improve their work. The readings in this lesson are examples. Workers can better understand their reading when they find the supporting details for the main idea.

1. Think about the material that you read at home, at work, and in school. How can finding the supporting details for a main idea make you a better reader?

Finish the sentence below.

Finding supporting details will help improve my reading because

2. Think about materials that you have read on a job. What did you read? Why was finding the supporting details important to understanding that reading?

Write a paragraph based on the questions above.

Check your answers on page 114.

Doing Research in Farming

Words to Know

agriculture

chemicals

crop rotation

erosion

fertilizers

pests

pesticides

soil

Suppose you work on a corn farm. Your boss plants the same amount of corn each year. But each year less corn grows. What may be causing this to happen? What can be done to fix it? How do you begin to look for answers?

Farmers and their employees face many problems like these. To find answers, they do research. *Research* is "careful study about a subject." They talk to experts and read about plants and farming.

In this lesson, you'll read some materials that farmers and farm employees might read. Some are books and other materials written by experts such as plant scientists.

Finding the main idea can help you better understand any material that you read. But often, the main idea of a reading is not stated. To **find an unstated main idea,** it helps to have a plan. In this lesson, you'll learn a strategy that can help you.

Job Focus

A **farm crew supervisor** is in charge of a group, or crew, of farm workers. He or she tells them what jobs to do. He or she makes sure the crew does work safely and correctly. A farm crew supervisor also shows workers how to do different tasks.

Usually, a farm crew supervisor takes care of paperwork. He or she may have to drive the crew to the fields. Some farmers have the farm crew supervisor hire the temporary workers during busy times.

The U.S. government reports that farms are becoming larger and more technical (TEHK-nih-kuhl). There is a need for farm supervisors who have reading skills. Being a farm crew supervisor is a step toward becoming a farm manager.

Finding an Unstated Main Idea: How It Works

A writer may not state the main idea. You can **find an unstated main idea** in a reading. Here's a strategy that can help you:

1. Read the whole reading. Identify the general subject—the overall topic of the reading.
2. Study the paragraphs and their supporting details. Figure out the main idea of each paragraph.
3. Put the paragraphs together. Ask yourself, "What important idea do all the paragraphs support?" That's the main idea of the reading.

Now, try using the plan. Read the following example of information that a farm crew supervisor might read.

pests weeds, bugs, or animals such as mice or deer that can harm crops

---

Aphids—Corn

Corn leaf aphids. These bugs are one of the worst **pests** for corn farmers. The small corn leaf aphids are blue-green. They like to eat the top parts of corn. They spread onto the corn's tassels, upper leaves, and upper stalk (or main stem). They leave a sticky dew behind. This dew attracts other kinds of pests to the corn.

Corn root aphids. The corn root aphids look much like the corn leaf aphids. Ants carry these aphids underground. The corn root aphid spreads underground, eating at the corn stalk's roots. Corn root aphids also cause much damage to corn crops.

What is the *general* subject of the reading? The subject is *aphids that eat corn plants.* Read over the paragraphs. What is the main idea of each paragraph? The main idea of the first paragraph is *corn leaf aphids are one of the worst pests for corn farmers.*

The main idea of the second paragraph is *corn root aphids also cause much damage to corn crops.*

Now, think about the reading as a whole. What is the main idea?_____

    a. Aphids are bad for all types of crops.
    b. Two types of aphids cause problems for corn farmers.
    c. Farmers cannot control aphids in corn crops.

The correct answer is b. Both paragraphs support that idea, so it is the main idea.

Some universities have **agriculture** departments that do research on plants and farm problems. Sometimes, they write up their findings for farmers to read.

This reading is an example of a brochure (broh-SHOOR) that farmers might get. The brochure is about problems with **pesticides**. Read the brochure.

Safe Pest Control: For Humans and the Land

Since the 1950s, farmers have thought that pesticides made from **chemicals** are the best weapon against insect pests. But now, findings show that fewer pests are dying from these pesticides. Some studies report that pesticides have created other problems. Many pesticides do not break down quickly. They can stay around and harm the land and water supply, as well as humans and animals.

Using other insects

When pesticides are sprayed on a crop, they also kill "good insects"—bugs that eat the harmful pests. In the animal world, some animals eat other animals for food. So farmers can control pests by releasing "good insects" into fields. For example, some farmers release ladybugs in their corn fields to control aphids. The ladybugs eat the aphids.

Using natural pesticides

Farmers do not have to stop using all kinds of pesticides. Some natural pesticides control pests better than pesticides made by people. Natural pesticides are made from plants. They are less harmful to the land and water. And they're safe for humans and animals.

Using an old farm method

Another pest control method is **crop rotation.** Pests somehow remember where they can find their food source. Pests will return to the same field when the same crop—like corn—is planted year after year. Crop rotation provides less food, and in some years, no food, for the pests. Fewer pests appear as a result of rotation.

Answer each question based on the reading on page 20.

1. What is the general subject of the brochure?

   a. pests
   b. pesticides
   c. pest control

2. What is the main idea of the first paragraph?

   a. Pesticides kill weeds, bugs, and other pests.
   b. Pesticides are killing fewer pests and harming life and land.
   c. Farmers use more pesticides than they did in the 1950s.

3. What is the main idea of the second paragraph?

   a. Ladybugs can kill the pests that destroy crops.
   b. There are good and bad pests.
   c. Farmers can use good insects to control other pests.

4. What is the main idea of the third paragraph?

   a. Some pesticides are made from plants.
   b. Natural pesticides work better than chemicals.
   c. Natural pesticides are not as effective.
   d. Natural pesticides are safe and effective.

5. What is the main idea of the fourth paragraph?

   a. Farmers can use the crop rotation method to control pests.
   b. Crop rotation means always planting the same crop in the same field.
   c. Farmers no longer use the crop rotation method.
   d. Pests know where to find the crops they like to eat.

6. Now, figure out the main idea for the whole reading. What is the main idea of the whole brochure?

The main idea is

Check your answers on page 114.

My name is Will. I've been working for Mr. Morgan almost 16 years. He owns a produce farm. A few years ago, Mr. Morgan made me his farm crew supervisor. I supervise eight workers.

I like my job. Mr. Morgan tells me that I'm good at telling people what to do. He says that I am also a good teacher.

As a supervisor, I have to do a lot of paperwork. At the beginning, it was tough to do. I couldn't read well.

One day, my son told me about a group that teaches adults to read. "What did I have to lose?" I asked myself. So I signed up. I'm glad I did. My reading improved a lot. The paperwork isn't so hard to do anymore.

Reading has helped me learn a lot about farming. Right now, my boss is thinking about changing his way of farming. He wants to do sustainable (suh-STAYN-uh-buhl) farming. This is a way of farming that does not harm the land. After Mr. Morgan explained it to me, he said, "Will, it's how our grandparents used to farm. With their heads and hearts."

We both laughed. We think it's a good idea.

Mr. Morgan gets books and magazines about sustainable farming. He reads them first, then gives them to me to read. We talk about what we read. When we don't understand, we ask the experts at the farm bureau or the university.

Today, the boss and I are going to visit another farm. The farmer has been doing sustainable farming for a few years. We want to hear first-hand what he thinks.

TALK ABOUT IT

1. Describe one thing that Will might read on the job.

2. Explain why Will needed to improve his reading.

F arm crew supervisors might read books about different farming subjects. On this page is an example of reading from a book on farming. Read the selection.

Protecting Farmland

soil the dark, rich top layer of dirt that plants grow in

Scientists report that every year, thousands of tons of **soil** are lost. It takes hundreds of years to build up healthy soil that is rich enough for plants to grow in.

How are we losing rich farmlands?

erosion (ih-ROH-zhuhn) a loss of dirt caused by wind or water

Erosion is natural. When soil is not protected, wind and rain carry it away. Some farming practices can cause more erosion than usual. One such practice is the use of heavy machines. More farmers use machines for plowing, planting, removing weeds, and harvesting crops. Over the years, land gets packed down. When it rains, the soil cannot soak up the rain. Instead, the rain carries the soil away.

The breakdown of soil into dust is also natural. On its own, this soil breakdown would take many years. Some soil experts find that chemical pesticides and **fertilizers** make the soil break down faster. The soil then turns into dust that gets picked up by the wind.

Farming practices also cause the loss of soil quality. Crops need food in soil to grow. Year after year of planting in the same soil strips the soil of food. To make sure plants will grow, farmers spread fertilizers on their crops.

How can farmers keep farmlands healthy and safe?

Farmers can take action to protect farmlands. Here are a few things they can do:
○ Plow the land so that the soil does not become solidly packed.
○ Use natural fertilizers that break down and feed the soil.
○ Leave plant stubble in the fields after harvesting the crops. The leftover plants protect the soil from wind and rain.
○ Practice crop rotation. Plant different crops in different years. This helps build up the soil.
○ Plant a cover crop during the winter. This will keep soil from being washed away during the rain. In the spring, the crop can be plowed into the earth. This is good for the soil.

fertilizers (FER-tl-eye-zuhrz) plant foods that are added to the soil to help crops grow

Farming practices

19

Answer each question based on the reading on page 23.

1. What is the general subject of the reading?

2. What is the main idea of the first paragraph?

3. What is the main idea of the second and third paragraphs? (State one main idea that applies to both paragraphs.)

4. What is the main idea of the fourth paragraph?

5. What is the main idea of the last paragraph?

6. Study your answers for questions 2 through 5. Write a sentence that states the main idea of the reading.

Check your answers on page 114.

◆ LESSON WRAP-UP

In this lesson, you learned a strategy that can help you find the unstated main idea of a reading. The strategy is:

1. **Read the whole reading.** Ask yourself, "What is the general subject?"
2. **Study the paragraphs and their supporting details.** Ask yourself, "What is the main idea of each paragraph?"
3. **Put the reading together as a whole.** Ask yourself, "What main idea do all the paragraphs support?"

Farm crew supervisors often read materials that have an unstated main idea. You've read examples of those materials in this lesson. A worker who does research on a subject will read many different materials. So it's important to be able to find an unstated main idea. When workers don't know the main idea, they may not understand what they're reading.

1. Suppose you're reading an office memo at your job. It explains a new procedure (a set of steps) for doing time cards. The main idea of the memo is not stated. Why should you find the main idea of that memo?

Finish the sentence below.

I should find the main idea of the memo because

2. Think about a time when you had a hard time reading something at work. What was the job? What were you reading? What was the problem? How would finding the main idea have helped you?

Write a paragraph based on the questions above.

Check your answers on page 114.

FINDING AN UNSTATED MAIN IDEA

1. What is meant by the main idea of a reading?

2. What is meant by a supporting detail?

3. If a main idea of a reading is not stated, how can you find what it is?

4. Think of the jobs that you learned about in this unit. Which one would you be interested in doing or learning more about? Why are you interested in this job? How could you learn more about it? Why would it be important to have strong reading skills for this job?

Write a paragraph based on these questions.

Check your answers on page 114.

Jobs Working with Animals

People work with animals in the country, in the city, and in the suburbs. They work at farms, ranches, zoos, aquariums, pet shops, kennels, pet hospitals, and animal shelters. Some jobs involve taking care of animals while other jobs focus on training them. Some jobs involve raising animals for food. Other jobs provide people with information about animals. And other jobs involve selling animals.

People working with animals read different kinds of materials. Workers read some materials, such as work schedules, to remind them what jobs to do and when to do them. They read materials such as animal guidebooks to help them learn about the animals that they work with. You will learn about some of these materials in this unit.

This unit teaches the following reading skills:

◆ making inferences
◆ comparing and contrasting
◆ classifying information

You will learn how people who work with animals use these reading skills.

Taking Care of Pets

Suppose you work in a pet shop. You get this note from your boss. The note gives a work instruction.

> The goldfish food section needs to be stocked. Please put more boxes out on the shelf today.

Work instructions are one type of material that pet care assistants read on the job. Pet care assistants read books and magazines to learn more about pets. They read brochures and advertisements (ad-vuhr-TEYEZ-muhnts) to learn more about pet products. In this lesson, you'll read materials related to taking care of pets.

Sometimes workers find that some ideas are unstated in a reading. But by **making inferences** (IHN-fuhr-uhns-uhz), they can figure out those unstated ideas. In this lesson, you will learn how to make inferences about what you read.

Job Focus

Pet care assistants must know about the animals that pet shops sell. Fish, birds, cats, dogs, turtles, snakes, lizards, mice, guinea pigs, and rabbits are some of the animals sold in pet shops.

Pet care assistants feed and water pets as well as wash and exercise them. They clean cages, sweep floors, and dust shelves. They might put stock on shelves and make store displays. They might also help customers and work the cash register.

Pet care assistants work in pet kennels, pet supply stores, pet-sitting services, pet grooming services, and pet training schools. This job group is expected to grow in the next few years because more people will own pets.

Making Inferences: How It Works

Authors often don't write every detail about a subject. They leave out ideas that readers already know or can figure out. Good readers use clues from their reading to find unstated ideas.

When you figure out unstated ideas in a reading, you're **making inferences.** You'll think of some unstated ideas right away. With other unstated ideas, you'll need to study carefully the details that are stated.

Here are two things you can do to help make inferences:

- Think about the subject. What do you already know about it? Your knowledge can give you clues to the unstated ideas.
- Study the main idea and the details. What clues do they give you about the unstated idea?

Below is an advertisement that pet care assistants might read in a magazine. Now, practice making inferences. Read the ad, and try to imagine the product.

What kind of product is the ad for?

_____

    a. a book for keeping pictures of a pet cat
    b. a book for writing notes about a pet cat

The answer is b. If you have knowledge about cat-sitting, you have a clue to the unstated idea. Most cat owners leave a long note about their cat. The note would include feeding instructions and what to do if the cat gets sick or hurt.

The main idea of the ad is a clue: *With* The Meow Manual, *your cat-sitter will know every detail about your precious cat.*

The details in the ad are clues, too. It says that the cat-sitter will know about food, allergies, medicines, and the vet.

Put all the clues together to make an inference about the product: It is a book for writing notes about a pet cat.

Customers at pet shops often ask for tips about taking care of pets. So pet care assistants learn about this subject. They read newspaper or magazine columns written by pet experts. Here is an example. Read the column.

Dr. Nick's Pet Notes

SEIZE THOSE FLEAS!

With summer coming, I have received many letters about fleas. Many ask the same questions. Here are some answers.

■ *Why do fleas bite my pet and me?*

That's where fleas find their food—blood. A bite is the result of a flea pricking the skin of an animal and sucking up the blood.

■ *Where do fleas live?*

Fleas live on animals. And once they're in your home, they live mostly in the cracks and corners of rooms and closets. You can also find them "hanging out" in rugs, upholstery, bedding, and even clothing.

■ *How do I keep fleas from getting on my pets and in my home?*

That's tough. Your pet and home might escape fleas if you keep your pet indoors during the hot seasons.

■ *How can I get rid of fleas?*

Repeat the following steps every week until you are sure the fleas are gone:
1. Bathe your pet—outdoors if possible! You don't want those fleas escaping into your bathroom rug. Afterwards, apply flea powder or spray on your pet. Or have your pet wear a flea collar. But don't do both. That can be poisonous to your pet.
2. Wash your pet's bedding in hot, soapy water. Dry it in the sun.
3. Thoroughly vacuum every room and closet in your house. Throw the vacuum bag out immediately! You might want to apply a flea powder or spray around baseboards.

For a bad case of fleas, **fumigate** your home. Use a flea bomb once a week for three weeks. It's not safe for you or your pet to breathe the fumes from the flea bomb. Be sure to follow the safety instructions on the product.

---

fumigate (FYOO-mih-gayt) to kill insects with a gas or smoke

LESSON 4 ◆ TAKING CARE OF PETS

These items ask you to make inferences based on the reading on page 30. Each item has two statements. Put an X by the statement that you think is correct and explain why.

Example

A flea would look for food on a

    a. tomato plant.

X b. rabbit.

This is correct because *fleas suck blood from humans and animals for food.*

1. The weather turns hot. Your cat begins to scratch much more than usual. What should you do?

    a. You should assume the cat has fleas and bathe her right away.

    b. You should leave the cat alone and wait for fleas to bite you.

This is correct because

2. You're about to fumigate your home for fleas. Is it safe for you and your pet to stay in the house?

    a. Yes, it's safe for my pet and me to stay.

    b. No, my pet and I should leave the house while fumigating.

This is correct because

3. You have just vacuumed your house for fleas. You should throw the vacuum bag away because

    a. the fleas may escape from the bag.

    b. the bag is probably full.

This is correct because

4. If you take your dog to the park every day, your dog will probably

    a. get fleas during the summer.

    b. get fleas during the winter.

This is correct because

Check your answers on page 115.

Kelly is nineteen years old. She works full time at her aunt's pet shop. She's been working there for three years.

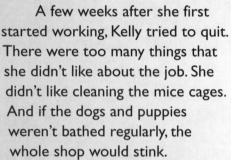

A few weeks after she first started working, Kelly tried to quit. There were too many things that she didn't like about the job. She didn't like cleaning the mice cages. And if the dogs and puppies weren't bathed regularly, the whole shop would stink.

Kelly also didn't like it when customers asked questions about their pets. She didn't know any answers, so she felt dumb.

The day that Kelly told her aunt she was quitting, her aunt asked why. Kelly told her. Her aunt said, "I can't do anything about how the animals smell. But I can help you learn about animals. Then, you can tell customers what they want to know."

Kelly agreed to stay for six months. If she still didn't like it, she could go. Later, her aunt showed Kelly the small library in her office. She said, "I learned most of what I know about the pets I sell from these books. They might help you, too."

Kelly groaned. She didn't like reading. But she had made a bargain with her aunt. At first, Kelly looked only at the pictures in the books. But soon she wanted to know more about the pictures.

Every week, Kelly would pick an animal and learn about it. She read whenever she could. She read after feeding the animals and cleaning their cages. She read before stocking the shelves. She read between helping customers.

One day, Kelly had a long talk with a customer who had lizards for pets. She gave suggestions about taking care of them. She also suggested some books to read. As he left, the customer said, "You're really helpful, Kelly. Thanks a lot!"

TALK ABOUT IT

1. Describe some of the materials that Kelly read on her job.

2. Has reading on her job improved Kelly's reading?

P et care assistants can get useful information about animals from posters. Here's an example of a poster that they might read. Read the poster.

Cats Are What They Eat!

Cats are a lot like us. To stay healthy, cats need a well-balanced diet. Every day, your cat should eat a variety of foods. Give your cat both fresh and packaged foods. Make sure your pet gets the right amount of **nutrients**.

◇ **Starches and Sugars.** Beans, grains (such as rice and barley), and vegetables have these nutrients. They give your cat get-up-and-go energy. They also help keep your cat's **digestion** healthy and in working order.

◇ **Proteins.** You'll find these nutrients in meats, eggs, and milk. Proteins are needed for your cat's growth. With some kinds of illnesses, proteins help a sick cat heal itself.

◇ **Fats.** Fats are needed for healthy fur. They also transport the fat-**soluble** vitamins (A, D, E, and K) throughout your pet's body. Most cats get all the fats they need. These nutrients are found in meats and milk. Only older cats need any extra fat. Feed older cats up to one teaspoon every day.

◇ **Vitamins and Minerals.** Without these nutrients, the body can't use the proteins, starches, and fats in food properly. Vitamins and minerals help keep your cat's body strong and healthy. Your cat will get the right amounts if it's eating a healthy variety of foods.

◇ **Water.** Yes, water is a nutrient. Make sure your cat gets plenty of fresh water throughout the day.

To answer each question, make an inference based on the poster on page 33.

1. What might happen if a cat did not eat enough starches and sugars?

2. What nutrients would a cat get from eating chicken?

3. Is it a good idea to feed tuna fish to a cat at every meal? Why or why not?

4. Might feeding chicken to a sick cat help it get better? Why or why not?

5. Suppose you mix corn, rice, peas, and liver together. Would that be a balanced meal for a cat? Why or why not?

6. If a cat doesn't drink enough water, what do you think might happen to it?

7. Suppose a cat is not as active as it used to be. Should you continue feeding it the same amount of food? Why or why not?

Check your answers on page 115.

◆ LESSON WRAP-UP

In this lesson, you learned how to make inferences from a reading. You make inferences about ideas that an author leaves out. An author leaves out ideas that readers are likely to know or figure out.

You learned how clues help you make inferences. Your knowledge and experience about a subject provide some clues. The ideas in a reading are other clues.

In this lesson, you read some materials that pet care assistants might read. Often, they read magazines, newspapers, books, and other things to learn more about taking care of pets. Making inferences can help workers understand the materials that they read.

1. Think about the material that you read at home, at work, and in school. How will it help improve your reading if you make inferences?

Finish the sentence below.

Making inferences can help improve my reading because

2. Think about materials that you have read on a job. What was the job? What did you read? How did making inferences help you better understand what you read on the job?

Write a paragraph based on the questions above.

Check your answers on page 115.

Working at a Zoo

▼▼▼▼▼▼▼▼▼▼▼

Words to Know

domestic

flock

mate

origin

withers

Have you ever taken a tour at a zoo? Or have you ever visited a pet kennel or a horse stable or even an animal shelter? Maybe you asked some questions about the different animals.

You may have noticed that the workers at these places know a lot about the different animals. As animal caretakers, they need to know a lot of details about the animals they care for. They may learn some things from co-workers or their employers. But most workers probably learn about animals by reading materials on the job.

In this lesson, you'll read materials that animal caretakers in zoos read. Some materials that they read are employee handbooks, animal guidebooks, and information sheets.

It's important that animal caretakers understand what they read. **Comparing and contrasting** details can help them understand information about different animals. You'll learn about this reading skill in this lesson.

Job Focus

A **zookeeper assistant** has several tasks. They include preparing food, feeding and watering the animals, and cleaning the animals' quarters. A zookeeper assistant might also keep watch for animal illnesses and injuries. He or she might also give tours and answer visitors' questions about the animals.

The job market for animal caretakers is expected to grow in the next few years. Many jobs will include those that train workers who have little or no work experience. But getting zookeeper assistant jobs or other zoo animal caretaker jobs may be hard. There is always heavy competition for these jobs.

Comparing and Contrasting: How It Works

Sometimes, authors write about two or more subjects together. They may show how the subjects are alike and different. When they **compare** details, they show how the subjects are alike. When they **contrast** details, they show how the subjects are different.

For example, on this page is a description of an animal. A zookeeper assistant might read this in an animal guidebook. Read the description.

Llama—A Relative of the Camel

The llama (pronounced *LAH muh*) is part of the camel family. It lives in the high mountains of South America, while the camel lives in the deserts of Africa and Asia.

Llamas are smaller than camels. Llamas stand about four feet tall at the shoulders. Camels are about two to three feet taller. Llamas' bodies—like camels'—have long, thick hair. But unlike camels, llamas have no hump on their backs.

The llama, like the camel, is a **domestic** animal. Humans have used both animals for food and clothing. They are particularly useful as pack animals. Llamas can carry over 100 pounds on their back and walk between 15 to 20 miles a day with a load.

---

domestic (duh-MEHS-tihk) bred for human use, such as for food or work

What is the subject? What is it being compared to? Why is it being compared to that animal? *The description is about an animal called a llama. It is being compared to a camel because they are both of the same family.*

Read the description again. Compare the details. How are the animals alike? By comparing details, you would find that the llama and camel are alike in these ways: *They are of the same animal family. They have long, thick hair. Humans use both animals for food, clothing, and as pack animals.*

Look over the description again. Now contrast the details. How are the animals different?

_____

_____

The animals are different in these details: *where they live, how big they are, and whether or not they have a hump on their backs.*

There are two ways to compare and contrast two subjects. One way is to give details for one subject first, then give details for the other subject. The second way is to cover the details for both subjects at the same time.

Read the description again. How did the writer discuss the details? *The writer used the second method— covering both subjects at the same time.*

Zookeeper assistants might read information about animals from an employee handbook. Here's an example of a description that they might find there. Read the description.

origin (AHR-uh-jihn) the place where something or someone came from

withers (WIHTH-uhrz) the part between the shoulder blades on a horse's back

---

Animals at the Children's Zoo

The Pony and the Donkey

The pony and the donkey are smart, gentle, and like to be around people. They belong to the same animal family— the horse family. The **origin** of the pony is Asia. The origin of the donkey, experts say, is in Africa. For over 5,000 years, the donkey and the pony have been domestic animals.

The Pony

A pony is a small horse. Its average height is 56 inches at its **withers**. The pony's body differs from a horse's in two ways. The pony has a deeper back. And its legs are shorter compared to its body size. Otherwise, a pony looks the same as a horse.

Like the horse, a pony is used for pleasure riding and for races. People have used ponies as pack animals as well. Ponies have the strength to carry heavy loads over long distances.

Ponies are smart animals. They can be trained to obey commands. Pony owners describe their pets as charming, lively, trusting, and loving.

The Donkey

The donkey is smaller than the pony. Its average height is 44 inches at its withers. It has the same shape as the horse. But its features are quite different. A donkey has longer ears. It has a short mane that stands up on its neck. Its body is usually gray with a dark line across its back.

Donkeys are strong and sure-footed. Throughout history, they have been used to carry heavy packs over mountains and deserts. Light, speedy donkeys have been used for riding.

Donkeys are often thought of as stubborn animals. But most donkey owners describe them as sweet and friendly.

Circle the correct answer based on the reading on page 38. If a statement is false, explain why that statement is false.

Example

True (False) The donkey and the pony are names for the same animal.

The statement is false because the donkey and the pony are two different animals.

True   False   1. Donkeys and ponies belong to a different family.

True   False   2. Donkeys and ponies have the same origin.

True   False   3. The pony and donkey are smaller than the horse.

True   False   4. Donkeys and ponies do not make good pets for children because they are too stubborn.

True   False   5. Donkeys are used only for carrying packs, and ponies are used only for riding.

Check your answers on page 115.

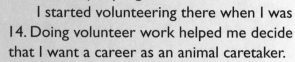

I'm a zookeeper assistant at the Lincoln Children's Zoo. This is my second summer working there as part of the summer job program.

I started volunteering there when I was 14. Doing volunteer work helped me decide that I want a career as an animal caretaker.

My friends are always saying, "Nadia, aren't you afraid of getting bitten?" I just shake my head. I tell them, "I'm only working with domestic animals—farm animals."

You'll find only domestic animals at this children's zoo. The zoo is busiest on the weekends. That's when a lot of families come to see the animals. Many kids have never seen or touched a live animal before. I like the way kids giggle and smile when an animal eats from their hand. It's a bonus to me to see the kids so happy.

One of my jobs is to feed the animals. I like to feed the llama, donkey, goat, and pony. They're very gentle creatures. I don't care too much for feeding the chickens, turkeys, and geese. They make too much noise, and sometimes they peck at my ankles.

During visiting hours, I talk to the visitors. The kids ask a lot of questions. They want to know what the animals eat and what makes an animal so special. They ask about things like that.

At my first training session, the zookeeper gave me information about the animals. I thought I knew a lot about farm animals, so I didn't read any of it. Was I wrong! I couldn't answer one question during my first time at the zoo.

I made sure I did my homework before I went back. I became most interested in learning more about goats. Can you believe that the goat and cow are from the same animal family? I don't think they look alike at all. But that's what the experts say!

TALK ABOUT IT

1. Describe what Nadia read to get information on animals.

2. Why did Nadia need to read about the farm animals at the zoo?

Some zoos will write up information about the animals at their zoo. They give their employees this information to study. Here's an example of an information sheet that zookeeper assistants might read. Read the information sheet.

Chickens and Geese at the Zoo

Chickens and domestic geese are often found in petting zoos. Both types of birds have wings and feathers.

Different Feet
Chickens and geese have different feet. Geese have webbed feet like ducks. Chickens do not. They have long sharp claws for gripping branches and scratching the ground.

Eating Habits
Chickens and geese differ in what they eat and how they find food. Chickens are peckers. They scratch the ground for grains and seeds, then peck them open with their beaks. Geese are grazers. They use their flat bills with tooth-like edges to hunt and eat grass.

Mating Habits
Geese will choose a partner and **mate** for life. Chickens are different. A rooster (the male) usually mates with more than one hen (the female) in its lifetime.

Raising Their Young
Both the goose (the female) and gander (the male) care for their young. When a gosling (baby goose) hatches, it leaves the nest right away. Its parents stay nearby to keep it safe.

The hen takes care of its chicks. Chicks can peck at food from the moment they're born. But the mother hen must give them food at first and teach them how to search for it.

Flock Behavior
Both types of birds move together as a **flock**. As a group, they find food and protect each other.

Within a flock of geese or chickens, one bird will become the boss. That bird is first in the "pecking order." It gets first pick of food and water. It also gets first pick at nests and roosting places.

mate to join with a partner to produce and raise offspring

flock a group of animals that live, feed, or move together

Answer each question based on the information sheet on page 41.

1. What feature do chickens and geese have in common?

2. What two features are different between the goose and the chicken?

3. Compare the following things between geese and chickens:

   a. How do they eat?

   b. How long do they mate?

   c. Who takes care of the young?

   d. How do they act in a flock?

Check your answers on page 115.

In this lesson, you learned how to compare and contrast details. You found out how authors describe two or more subjects, showing how they are alike and different. When you find out what details are alike, you're comparing them. And when you find out what details are different, you're contrasting them.

Workers often need to compare and contrast details in the materials that they read. They might use this skill when they are learning more about a work subject. Comparing and contrasting details can also help them understand what work they must do and how it must be done.

1. Think about the material that you read at home, at work, and in school. How will it improve your reading if you compare and contrast details?

Finish the sentence below.

Comparing and contrasting details can improve my reading because

2. Think about the materials that you have read on a job. Think about a reading in which you needed to compare and contrast details. What was the job? What did you read? Why was it important to compare and contrast the details?

Write a paragraph based on the questions above.

Check your answers on page 116.

Working in a Veterinary Clinic

▼▼▼▼▼▼▼▼▼▼▼

Words to Know

boarders

maintenance

substitute

Many animal hospitals, pet clinics, and veterinary (VEHT-uhr-ih-nehr-ee) offices have workers who come at different times of the day. They also have tasks that must be done two or more times during a day. For example, they might need to feed animals two or three times daily.

Work schedules keep track of who is working when. They also help keep track of who does different tasks during the day. You'll read about some of these work schedules in this lesson. They are examples of what workers in an animal hospital, pet clinic, and veterinary office read.

Work schedules are just one type of table that workers read in a workplace. Tables are a way of **classifying**, or organizing, **information**. Understanding how a table is organized is important for workers. In this lesson, you'll learn about classifying information in tables and how to get information from them.

Job Focus

In this lesson, you will read work schedules related to the job of **veterinary assistant.** You would find this job in an animal hospital, animal clinic, and veterinary office. This job also goes by the title veterinary attendant.

Veterinary assistants prepare food and medicines for animals. They feed and give water to animals and exercise them. They might clean examining rooms, cages, and operating rooms. They might also help the vet during office visits, home visits, and surgery (SER-juh-ree).

The U.S. government reports that jobs are expected to increase in the area of animal health care. These jobs include veterinarians (veht-uhr-ih-NEHR-ee-uhnz), veterinary technicians (tehk-NIHSH-uhnz), and veterinary assistants. They can be found in zoos, animal parks, and circuses. Also, jobs can be found in animal shelters, kennels, and animal labs.

Jobs will increase especially in animal hospitals, animal clinics, and veterinary offices. This is due to the growing number of pet owners who want good health care for their pets.

Classifying Information: How It Works

Sometimes, an author puts details into rows and columns to make a table. That is one way an author may **classify information** for easier reading. Classifying information is putting details that are alike into categories, or groups.

To get information from a table, follow these steps:

1. Figure out the purpose of the table. Read the title. What information does the table contain?
2. Figure out the categories. Read the headings across the top and down the left side. Every piece of information in the table is labeled up above by its column heading. It's labeled across by its row heading.
3. Find information in the table by following the rows and columns. To locate the fact you want, you look at where a row and a column meet.

The table on this page is a work schedule. It's one that a veterinary assistant might read. Read the table.

Tasks	Morning Shift	Afternoon Shift
Feed and exercise patients	Pat	Roy
Work in front office	Jessie	Pat
Help doctor with patients	Pat	Jessie

Vet Clinic Work Assignments

What is the purpose of the table? What is the title? The purpose of the table is *to show the work assignments in the clinic.*

What categories are the details classfied in?

_____

The row headings tell you which tasks the workers will do. The column headings tell you when (morning or afternoon).

Now, locate a detail in the table. Which employee will feed and exercise patients in the mornings?_____

First, look under the *Tasks* column. Find the task— *feed and exercise patients*. Then look across that row at the *Morning Shift* column. Where do the column and the row meet? The answer is *Pat*.

Which employee will help the doctor in the afternoon?

_____

The answer is *Jessie*.

Which employee will work in the front office at 4 p.m.?

_____

The answer is *Pat*.

An animal hospital or clinic needs employees to work different shifts. Workers might take turns on different shifts. Here's an example of how a work schedule might look at an animal clinic. Read the table.

New Town Pet Clinic Daily Work Shifts

Work Shift	Veterinarian	Veterinary Technician	Veterinary Assistant
7 A.M. to 3 P.M.	Dr. Nhu	Tomas	Keisha Moses
1 P.M. TO 9 P.M.	Dr. Boyd	Lynn	Rhon Angela
9 A.M. TO 6 P.M. (WEEKENDS ONLY)	Dr. Willits	May Lee	Mark

LESSON 6 ◆ WORKING IN A VETERINARY CLINIC

Answer each question based on the reading on page 46.

1. What is the purpose of the table?

   a. To find out who is coming to work on time.
   b. To keep track of when people are listed to work.

2. What detail is *not* classified on the table?

   a. When each veterinary assistant works.
   b. What tasks each employee does.

3. Which veterinarian works the 7 A.M. to 3 P.M. shift.

   a. Dr. Boyd
   b. Dr. Nhu

4. Which veterinary assistant works in the 1 P.M. to 9 P.M. shift?

   a. Keisha
   b. Angela

5. Which veterinary technician works on Sundays?

   a. May Lee
   b. Mark

6. Suppose Lynn went on vacation for a week. What work shift would need to be filled that week?

   a. Veterinary Assistant, 7 A.M. TO 3 P.M.
   b. Veterinary Technician, 1 P.M. TO 9 P.M.

7. Mrs. Chang is the receptionist. She will be out of the office the week of June 1. Who would be able to fill in for her from 9 A.M. TO 12 P.M.?

   a. Angela
   b. Moses

8. Who would be likely to feed patients their evening meals on Tuesdays?

   a. Mark
   b. Rhon

Check your answers on page 116.

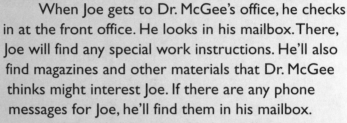

Joe Saeyang is a veterinary assistant. He works part time for Dr. McGee. Joe also works at the public library. But if he could, he would like to work full time for Dr. McGee.

When Joe gets to Dr. McGee's office, he checks in at the front office. He looks in his mailbox. There, Joe will find any special work instructions. He'll also find magazines and other materials that Dr. McGee thinks might interest Joe. If there are any phone messages for Joe, he'll find them in his mailbox.

Joe has a daily routine. He has tasks that he must do every day. First, he checks the cages to see if any animals need water. Next, he cleans up the cages. Then, he sweeps the floors and takes out the garbage. It doesn't take him long to do all that.

His biggest task usually takes up most of his time. He must exercise the dogs. Some dogs are healing from surgery. Others are boarders (BAWR-duhrz), which are pets that stay somewhere away from home while their owners are away. All the dogs need to get exercise every day unless they have just had surgery.

Joe usually takes two or three dogs at a time. They go to a park nearby. Joe walks or runs the dogs around the park. The job has helped Joe get into good shape.

Since he's been working at the clinic, Joe has learned a lot about dogs. He didn't realize how many different kinds there are. Bulldogs, beagles, poodles, Irish setters, basset hounds, and collies are a few of the dogs that he has learned about. Joe has also learned how different dogs are from each other.

Lately, Joe has been learning about jobs working with dogs. He likes the idea of training dogs for deaf and blind people or for the police. He could see himself enjoying that job.

TALK ABOUT IT

1. Describe some materials that Joe would read on his job.

2. Discuss how these reading materials might help Joe on his job.

Work schedules change from time to time. Workers might get a memorandum with a new work schedule. Here's an example of a memo that veterinary assistants might read. Read the memo.

boarders (BAWR-duhrz) pets that get meals and a place to stay while their owners are away from home

substitute (SUHB-stih-toot) someone who is taking the place of another

maintenance (MAYN-tuh-nuhns) work that must be done regularly, such as cleaning

---

New Town Pet Clinic

MEMORANDUM

TO: All Employees   Date: June 15
FROM: Mrs. Chang
SUBJECT: New Work Schedule

Dr. Boyd has asked me to make up a summer work schedule for taking care of patients and **boarders**. It will be for the months of July through September. The schedule will start July 1.

Please note the following: Morning meals should be given between 7 a.m. and 8 a.m. During weekdays, evening meals should be given between 6 p.m. and 7 p.m. On weekends, evening meals should be given between 4 p.m. and 5 p.m.

If you have to miss work, please tell me right away. I must tell your **substitute** to cover the necessary tasks.

If there are any problems with the schedule, please talk to me as soon as possible.

Day	Meals		Exercise Dogs		Maintenance
	A.M.	P.M.	A.M.	P.M.	
Monday	Keisha	Mark	Rhon	Lynn	Tomas
substitute	Dr. Boyd	Lynn	Keisha	Mark	Mark
Tuesday	Keisha	Mark	Rhon	Lynn	Tomas
substitute	Dr. Boyd	Lynn	Keisha	Mark	Mark
Wednesday	Keisha	Mark	Rhon	Lynn	Tomas
substitute	Dr. Boyd	Lynn	Keisha	Mark	Mark
Thursday	Keisha	Lynn	Keisha	Tomas	Rhon
substitute	Dr. Boyd	Mark	Rhon	Lynn	Tomas
Friday	Keisha	Lynn	Keisha	Tomas	Rhon
substitute	Dr. Boyd	Mark	Rhon	Lynn	Tomas
Saturday	Moses	Angela	Moses	Angela	Moses
substitute	Angela	Moses	Angela	Moses	Angela
Sunday	Moses	Angela	Moses	Angela	Moses
substitute	Dr. Willits	Moses	Angela	Moses	Angela

CHECK YOUR UNDERSTANDING

Answer each question based on the reading on page 49.

1. What is the purpose of the table?

2. What does the category "Maintenance" mean?

3. Which two categories show details for the morning and afternoon?

4. Cleaning cages and sweeping floors in the examining rooms are part of Rhon's duties on Thursday. If he's absent, who does it instead?

5. Who takes the dogs out for a walk on Friday mornings?

6. Who is supposed to feed the animals in the evenings on Wednesday and Thursday?

7. What time should the animals be fed on Tuesday evening?

8. Who would Dr. Willits substitute for on Sunday morning? What task would she be responsible for?

9. Suppose Keisha did not show up for work on Friday. Who would be her substitute for

   a. feeding the patients and boarders?
   b. exercising the dogs?

Check your answers on page 116.

◆ LESSON WRAP-UP

In this lesson, you learned about classifying information. When a subject has many details, an author may put details that are alike into categories. The author might classify the information in a table. To use a table, decide what piece of information you need. Then find it by looking for the point where the row and column meet.

In the workplace, workers read many tables. Some of them are work schedules such as the ones you read in this lesson. Understanding how information is classified will help you read tables.

1. Think of the tables that you have read at home, at work, and in school. How will it help you improve your reading if you understand how the details on a table are classified?

Finish the sentence below.

Understanding how information is classified can help improve my reading because

2. Think of the tables that you have read on a job. What was the job? What were the tables for? Why was it important that you understand how the details were classified on the table?

Write a paragraph based on the questions above.

Check your answers on page 116.

◆ UNIT TWO REVIEW

1. How do you make inferences from a reading?

2. When you compare and contrast details in a reading, what do you find out?

3. How is information classified in a table?

4. In this unit, you learned about some agricultural jobs that work with animals. Which job are you interested in doing or learning more about? Why are you interested in this job? How could you find out more about it? Why would it be important for you to have strong reading skills for this job?

Write a paragraph based on these questions.

Check your answers on page 116.

Jobs Working with Plants

Horticulture is the science of growing plants. The jobs are many and different. Seed companies, flower stores, nurseries, and garden centers are a few of the places where you can find horticulture jobs. Some jobs involve producing seeds from plants. Other jobs involve producing plants from seeds. Many of the jobs involve selling plants.

Horticulture workers read many materials on their jobs. You will read some of these materials in this unit. Some materials, such as package labels and job manuals, describe how to do a certain job or how to use a certain product. Other materials that horticulture workers might read are handbooks and textbooks. From these, they can learn about plants and how to take care of them.

This unit teaches the following reading skills:

◆ understanding visual information
◆ identifying cause and effect
◆ following directions

You will learn how workers in horticulture use these reading skills in their work.

Working in Horticulture

▼▼▼▼▼▼▼▼▼▼▼▼

Words to Know

absorb

chlorophyll

fertilization

photosynthesis

pollen

pollinate

Suppose you work for a seed company. Here's part of a page from their seed catalog. How does the catalog describe this product?

Golden Girl. A small crookneck squash that's golden-yellow. It has a medium neck with a round bulb-like end. This plant grows easily. Its fruits are easy to pick.

The catalog uses words and a picture to describe the product. The picture helps readers understand the written description.

Many work materials have pictures, or other kinds of information. One kind of visual that workers read on the job is a diagram (DEYE-uh-gram). **Understanding visual information** is an important reading skill. Diagrams at work may be used to show how something looks. They also may help explain how something works.

In this lesson, you'll read some diagrams that are related to producing seeds. You'll learn a strategy in this lesson that can help you get information from diagrams.

Job Focus

Seed and greenhouse technicians (tehk-NIHSH-uhnz) put pollen on flowers to make them reproduce (ree-pruh-DOOS). Other tasks for technicians include planting seeds, watering plants, and removing weeds. Seed and greenhouse technicians might harvest fruits and seed pods and prepare seeds for packages.

The U.S. government reports that the market for jobs related to horticulture (HAWR-tih-kuhl-chuhr) is good. Most horticulture jobs are expected to increase in the next few years.

Understanding Visual Information: How It Works

Here's a strategy that can help you read a **diagram.**

1. Study the diagram carefully. Read everything that's on it.

Most diagrams contain these kinds of written information:

- The *title* states the subject of a diagram.
- Some diagrams also have a *caption* (KAP-shuhn). The caption is below the diagram. It tells you more details about the subject.
- The *labels* name the parts of a diagram. Usually the labels are in the diagram, next to the parts they name.

2. Figure out the purpose of the diagram. What does the diagram show? What does it help you to understand?

3. Identify the parts of the diagram.

On this page is a diagram that a seed technician might read in a plant book. Look at the diagram.

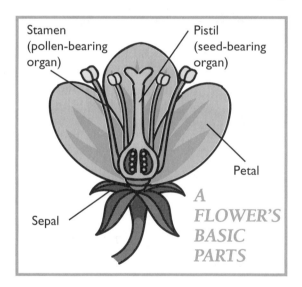

Stamen (pollen-bearing organ)

Pistil (seed-bearing organ)

Petal

Sepal

A FLOWER'S BASIC PARTS

The sepal, petal, stamen, and pistil are the main parts of a flower. One or more sepals on the outside of a flower protect the flower bud. They spread open as the flower blooms. The petals are the colorful parts of a flower. They protect a flower's reproductive ("sex") organs. These are the pistil and the stamen.

What is the title? What does the caption tell you? What do the labels name?

_____

_____

_____

The title is *A Flower's Basic Parts*. The caption tells you *more details about the parts*. The labels name *the parts of a flower*.

Now, read the diagram. What is its purpose?

_____

_____

The purpose of the diagram is *to show the parts of a flower*. Its parts are *the sepal, petal, pistil, and stamen*.

Seed research technicians might read diagrams like the one below to help them understand their work. They might find this diagram in a plant handbook. Read the diagram. Then, answer the questions on the next page.

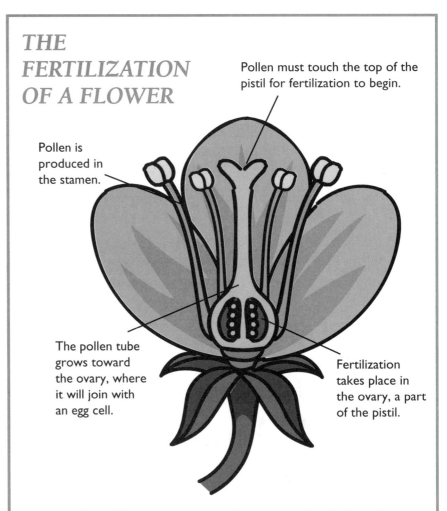

THE FERTILIZATION OF A FLOWER

Pollen must touch the top of the pistil for fertilization to begin.

Pollen is produced in the stamen.

The pollen tube grows toward the ovary, where it will join with an egg cell.

Fertilization takes place in the ovary, a part of the pistil.

From a plant's flower can come a fruit or seed pod. For this to happen, **fertilization** must take place. The process begins when birds and insects **pollinate** a flower.

For example, a butterfly sips nectar from a flower. Its body rubs against **pollen** on the stamen. The pollen clings to the insect. When the butterfly touches the top of a flower's pistil, some pollen rubs off on the pistil.

Fertilization starts when a pollen grain enters the pistil. The pollen grain grows a tube. This tube travels down the pistil toward the ovary. There, the tube joins with a female cell. That cell becomes a fertilized egg. It can grow into a fruit or a seed pod.

fertilization
(fer-tuhl-ih-ZAY-shuhn) the joining of a male cell and female cell to create a new living thing

pollinate (PAHL-uh-nayt) to put pollen on a flower to enable reproduction

pollen (PAHL-uhn) the male cells of a flower, which look like very fine, yellow dust

Answer each question based on the diagram on page 56.

1. What process does the diagram show as a whole?

   a. A flower dies when it's pollinated.
   b. The reproductive organs of a flower are the pistil and stamen.
   c. A male sex cell must join with an egg cell for fertilization to take place in a flower.
   d. Seeds grow inside the stamen.

2. Which statement describes a part of the diagram?

   a. A pollen grain unites with an egg cell in the ovary.
   b. Bees pick up pollen from the pistil.
   c. Stamens last only 24 hours.
   d. A flower can pollinate itself.

3. Which statement is true about the pistil?

   a. The pistil is where the male cells come from.
   b. Pollen is produced in the pistil.
   c. Pollen grains grow a tube inside the pistil.
   d. The ovary is at the top of the pistil.

4. Which is true about the stamen?

   a. Fertilization takes place in the stamen.
   b. Pollen travels down the stamen tube to the ovary.
   c. The stamen is where the pollen comes from.
   d. The stamen is always free of pollen.

5. Show the order of these steps in the fertilization of a flower. Write 1 for the first step. Write 2 for the second step, and so on. The first one is done for you.

   __ a. A pollen grain grows a tube and travels down the pistil.
   __ b. A pollen grain joins an egg cell in the ovary.
   __ c. Pollen touches the top of the pistil.
   _1_ d. An insect or bird rubs off pollen from the stamen.

Check your answers on page 117.

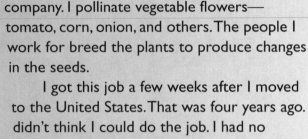

My name is Nataly. I'm a seed research technician at a big seed company. I pollinate vegetable flowers—tomato, corn, onion, and others. The people I work for breed the plants to produce changes in the seeds.

I got this job a few weeks after I moved to the United States. That was four years ago. I didn't think I could do the job. I had no experience. But Esperanza, my supervisor, said, "Nataly, if you're willing to learn, you can do anything."

It wasn't hard to learn this job. Whatever plant I work on, I do the same thing. I get pollen from the male part of a plant. Then I sprinkle it on the female part. But I do have to be careful. I can't let anything but pollen touch a pistil. I have to make sure that a pistil hasn't been pollinated by a bee or a or bug. And I use diagrams of flowers to be sure I pollinate the right plants.

The company has greenhouses, which are glass buildings where plants can be grown all year. Some plants are always ready for pollinating. Every day, Esperanza tells me which greenhouses to work in. She gives me greenhouse diagrams that show where the different plants are.

I carry a notebook where I write my assignments. That way, I make fewer mistakes. I write the names of the projects that I'm working on. My notebook helps me fill out my time card. I have to record the projects that I work on each week.

Last year, I took a plant science class. Now I better understand how plant breeding is done. I like to watch for the results. Someday I would like to have more responsibility for the work. So I'm learning everything I can. In the meantime, I practice my reading. I read books, magazines, anything!

TALK ABOUT IT

1. Describe two materials that Nataly would read on her job.

2. Discuss why reading more would help Nataly reach her goals.

Seed research technicians might read a diagram such as this one in a plant textbook. Read the diagram. Then, answer the questions on the following page.

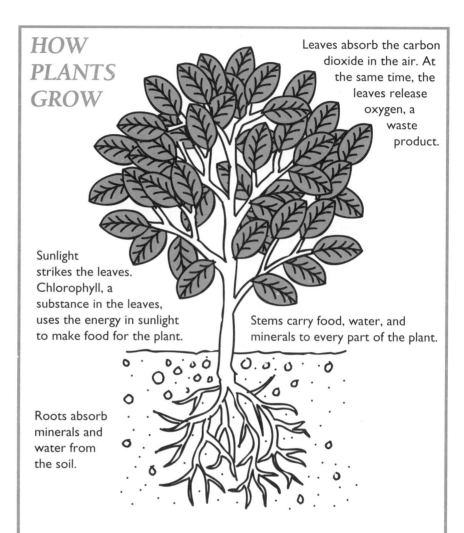

HOW PLANTS GROW

Leaves absorb the carbon dioxide in the air. At the same time, the leaves release oxygen, a waste product.

Sunlight strikes the leaves. Chlorophyll, a substance in the leaves, uses the energy in sunlight to make food for the plant.

Stems carry food, water, and minerals to every part of the plant.

Roots absorb minerals and water from the soil.

absorb (ab-ZAWRB) to take in a substance, such as when a sponge absorbs water

photosynthesis (foh-toh-SIHN-thuh-sihs) the process by which green plants use light energy to make their own food

chlorophyll (KLAWR-uh-fihl) the green coloring of plants, which plants use to make food

*For plants to grow and stay healthy, they need nutrients, such as minerals. Plants **absorb** minerals from the soil that they grow in. Water is also a nutrient for plants. Plants absorb water through their roots, stems, and leaves.*

*Plants, like all living things, need food. Unlike humans and animals, plants make their own food. Their food-making process is called **photosynthesis**. A plant's leaves catch sunlight. The energy in sunlight is used by **chlorophyll** to make food.*

A plant's leaves also take in and get rid of gasses. Plants need carbon dioxide, a gas, to stay healthy and alive. The leaves absorb carbon dioxide from the air. At the same time, the leaves release waste into the air. That waste is a gas called oxygen.

Answer each question based on the diagram on page 59.

1. What overall process does the diagram show?

2. What is the purpose of a plant's roots?

The purpose of a plant's roots is

3. What is the purpose of a plant's stems?

The purpose of a plant's stems is

4. A plant's leaves have two purposes. What are they?

    a. One purpose is

    b. One purpose is

5. How does a plant make its food?

6. Suppose a plant doesn't get enough essential nutrients. What might happen to the plant?

Check your answers on page 117.

In this lesson, you read some diagrams that a seed research technician might read. Diagrams help describe how something, such as a flower, looks. Diagrams also help explain how something works, such as how a flower grows.

You also learned in this lesson a strategy for reading diagrams. The strategy can help you understand a diagram and get information from it. The steps to the strategy are:

1. Study the diagram carefully. Read everything that's on it. Read the title, the caption, and the labels.
2. Figure out what the diagram shows as a whole.
3. Identify the parts of the diagram and how they relate to each other.

Diagrams are often part of materials that workers read on the job. In this lesson, you read some diagrams that would help seed research technicians do their work. The diagrams explained how plants are naturally fertilized and how plants grow.

1. Think about the diagrams that you read at home, at work, and in school. How will it help improve your reading if you can read diagrams?

Finish the sentence below.

Reading diagrams can improve my reading because

2. Think about diagrams that you have read on a job. What was the job? What did you read? Why was it important to understand the diagrams?

Write a paragraph based on the questions above.

Check your answers on page 117.

Selling Flowers

Working in a flower shop, you might read a sales form like this:

Date: *October 28*		No. 589782
Customer: *Liz Gold*		Phone Number: *555-1163*
Items		

1 bridal bouquet made of yellow, red, and white roses and baby's breath

3 women's corsages made of yellow roses

____ Pick up	Due: *November 15*
◊ Delivery: *567 Walnut Avenue / cross street 6th St.*	

Salesperson: *Sydney Juno*	Work by: _____

A sales form shows the details of a customer's order. In this lesson, you'll learn about other materials flower shop assistants read.

Many details in on-the-job readings are related. **Identifying cause and effect** among the details helps workers understand a reading. In this lesson, you'll learn this reading skill.

Job Focus

Flower shop assistants and **assistant florists** have different tasks. Some workers sell flowers and other products. Some workers set up flower displays or create flower arrangements. Some deliver flowers to customers.

The U.S. government reports that jobs in selling flowers and plants will grow in the next few years. This category includes flower shop jobs.

Identifying Cause and Effect: How It Works

Authors often write details that relate to each other in this way: one event causes another event to happen or take place. One event is a **cause**. It is the reason that something happens. The other event is an **effect**. It is the result of the cause.

Identifying cause and effect can help you understand a reading. To figure out a cause-and-effect relationship, ask yourself these questions:

- Why did something happen? Or, what is the *cause* that made an event happen?
- What happened? Or, what is the *effect* that happened as a result of the cause?

It's usually easier to look for the cause first, and then the effect. That's because the cause happens first.

Read the memo below.

docked (dahkt) reduced

> Date: December 15
> From: Kate Ferguson, Store Manager
>   To: Dolly Roberts
>   Dolly, you were warned on Monday about being late to work. You were told that your paycheck will be **docked** for the amount of time you are late.
>   On Tuesday, you were late to work 1 hour in the morning and 30 minutes from your lunch-break. Your pay will be docked for 1.5 hours of work you have missed.
>   This memo serves as your notice that if you are late two more times this month, you will be fired.

An effect in the memo is this: The worker's next paycheck will be smaller. What is the cause for that effect?

_____

a. She worked fewer days during that work period.
b. She was one-and-a-half hours late to work on Tuesday.

The answer is b. Because she was late 1.5 hours (*cause*), wages will be docked from her paycheck (*effect*).

Another effect in the memo is this: The employee can get fired. What would be the cause for that effect?

_____

The cause would be coming to work late two more times that month.

Here is an example of a memorandum, or memo, that a flower shop assistant might receive. Read the memo. Then, answer the questions on the next page.

❀ ❀ ❀ MEMORANDUM ❀ ❀ ❀

DATE: June 22
TO: All Employees Handling Flower Arrangements
FROM: Betty Warren
SUBJECT: Handling Dissatisfied Customers

Warren Flowers has been in the floral business for 50 years. Our store is well known for selling only the best and freshest flowers. But most of all, we are known for our friendly, efficient service.

From time to time, we get customers who are dissatisfied with their orders. When that happens, follow these instructions:

Customers have two choices.
Choice 1: Customers can get a **refund.** But they cannot keep the flower arrangement.
Choice 2: Customers may have their order done over.

How to Redo Orders
1. When customers choose to have an order done over, please explain our store policy. Make sure they understand this policy completely.

This is the policy: An order will be redone without any cost to the customer. If a customer is still dissatisfied with the redone order, a refund will not be given. If the customer wishes to have the order done again, he or she will be charged for it.
2. Use Form 58 for any redone orders. First, describe what is wrong with the flower arrangement that was made. Then, write up the customer's order. Have the customer sign the form. The customer must sign the form before an order can be redone.

If you have a problem with a customer, talk to the manager at once. The store manager will handle the dissatisfied customer.

refund (REE-fuhnd) money returned to a customer

Answer each question based on the memo on page 64. For questions 1–5, circle *True* if both the cause and effect are correct. Circle *False* if either the cause or effect is not correct.

Example

True (False)

Cause: A customer is dissatisfied with an order that has been redone.
Effect: The customer can ask the store to do it again without paying for it.

1. True   False

Cause: Warren Flowers provides good products and good service.
Effect: Warren Flowers is well known.

2. True   False

Cause: A customer doesn't like the way a Warren Flowers employee spoke to him.
Effect: The customer can get a refund.

3. True   False

Cause: A customer is dissatisfied with her flower arrangement.
Effect: She has to pay to get it done over.

4. True   False

Cause: Ms. Gee has asked to have her order redone.
Effect: A flower shop assistant fills out Form 58 for Ms. Gee's order.

5. True   False

Cause: Mr. Katz will not sign Form 58.
Effect: Mr. Katz cannot have his order done over.

6. Like Warren Flowers, many businesses have policies about giving customers refunds and redoing orders. What might cause businesses to need policies like these?

Check your answers on page 117.

Mrs. Warren owns several flower stands in the city. I work at the flower stand on Page and Filbert. It's near the business district. It's also near the big stores downtown. So I get a lot of customers.

My work day starts at 6:00 A.M. I go to the flower market. That's where flower growers bring their flowers to sell. I meet Jeannie there and help her buy flowers. She's the manager of my stand. She manages three other flower stands, too.

I like being at the flower market. Some flowers still have their morning dew on them. What I especially like is seeing all the beautiful colors of the different flowers. Pink. White. Blue. Yellow. You name the color, you can find it at the flower market.

I open the flower stand at 7:30 A.M. On Mondays, Jeannie helps me. She stays until 9:30 A.M.; then she goes to another stand. Frank, another worker, starts at 10:00 A.M. I get off work at 2:00.

Good hours, don't you think? I've been working those hours for over a year now. After work, I go to the community college. I'm taking a reading and writing class to improve my skills. I'm also taking a flower arrangement class.

Mrs. Warren pays for my college courses. That's one of my work benefits from her company. Mrs. Warren's a great boss. She thinks well of her employees. She is always helping us to improve ourselves.

I plan to stay with Mrs. Warren's company for a long time. I would like to be a manager like Jeannie.

I like every part of the flower business—selecting the flowers, setting up displays, serving customers. I even like doing the physical work and the paperwork. I dream that someday Warren Flowers will name its new president: James Chu. That's me!

TALK ABOUT IT

1. Describe two kinds of material that James might read on his job.

2. Why should James improve his reading and writing skills?

LESSON 8 ◆ SELLING FLOWERS

procedure (pruh-SEE-juhr) a series of steps to follow in order

Flower shop assistants follow a **procedure** for almost every task they do. Some flower stores may place these instructions in an employee manual.

Here's an example of a procedure that flower shop assistants might follow. Read the procedure. Then, answer the questions on the next page.

browse (browz) to look around

complimentary (kahm-pluh-MEHN-tuh-ree) offered by a store or business at no charge

---

Serving Customers at the Cordero Flower Stores

At Cordero Flowers, Inc., the customer is *always* right! All customers are to be treated the same way—with friendliness, respect, and politeness. Every person who comes into the shop is a customer. Even people who only **browse.**

All employees are expected to follow this procedure:

1. Welcome a customer.

   Welcome all customers with a friendly smile and greeting. Ask how you might help them. Answer their questions politely. Let customers take their time to browse around the store.

2. Wait on a customer.

   Help one customer at a time. Wait on customers in the order that they come up to you or come into the store. Let your manager know when more help is needed to wait on customers.

3. Prepare a customer's purchase.

   Wrap up the customer's purchase before ringing it up on the cash register. Be sure to show customers the display of **complimentary** greeting cards.

   Always assume that flowers are a special gift. Put complimentary ferns or other greens with the flowers. Use a matching gift wrap paper and ribbon to wrap them all together.

4. Ring up a customer's purchase.

   Customers may pay by cash, check, or credit card. If payment is made by credit card, make sure the customer signs the slip and gets the right part back.

5. Send customers away with a smile.

   Let the customers know that you appreciate their business. As they leave the counter or shop, wish them a cheerful "Good day." Also invite them to come back again.

Answer each question based on the procedure on page 67. Read each cause or effect. Then, fill in the missing cause or effect.

Example

Cause: There are many customers in the flower shop. She can't wait on them all.

Effect: A flower shop assistant finds the manager in the office. She says, "We need help out front."

1. *Cause:*

Effect: The flower shop assistant smiles at a customer. She says, "Hello. May I help you?"

2. *Cause:* A flower shop assistant shows a customer where the complimentary cards are.

Effect:

3. *Cause:* When a florist wraps up a customer's purchase, she assumes it will be a gift.

Effect:

4. *Cause:*

Effect: The customer signs a credit card slip.

5. *Cause:* "Have a good day!" says a flower shop assistant to a customer.

Effect:

Check your answers on page 117.

◆ LESSON WRAP-UP

In this lesson, you learned how to identify details that have a cause-and-effect relationship. A cause is the reason that something has happened. An effect is the result of what has happened.

Identifying cause and effect among details can help you understand a reading. You saw how this skill was helpful for understanding the job materials that flower shop assistants might read. This skill is especially helpful when workers need to follow procedures.

1. Think about the material that you read at home, at work, and in school. How will identifying cause and effect help you improve your reading?

Finish the sentence below.

Identifying cause and effect can improve my reading because

2. Think about materials that you have read on a job. What did you read? How did identifying cause-and-effect relationships help you understand what you read on the job?

Write a paragraph based on the questions above.

Check your answers on page 117.

Working in a Nursery

▼▼▼▼▼▼▼▼▼▼▼▼

Words to Know

germinate

potting soil

seedlings

sow

transplant

If you worked in a plant nursery, you might read this label:

Yard & Garden BUG Killer
Kills aphids, beetles, caterpillars, chinch bugs, thrips, whiteflies. Shake Well. Keep away from children.

A product's label gives information about the product. It may describe what a product is used for.

A package label is one kind of material that workers must read in the workplace. In this lesson, you'll read about directions for using products on the job. If workers can't understand directions they read on packages, they may not be able to complete their work.

Workers often must **follow directions** on their jobs. They must understand every step of the directions. In this lesson, you'll learn a strategy that can help you read and follow directions.

Job Focus

Nursery workers or **nursery technicians** work in a plant nursery. They might also work in a garden center in a large retail store.

Nursery workers have many tasks. They might maintain plants by watering and weeding them. They might plant seeds and plants in pots. They might put out new stock on shelves or set up plant displays. They might maintain the grounds. They might wait on customers and work the cash register.

Job openings for nursery workers are good. More people are interested in buying plants—indoor and outdoor—for their homes. These jobs will increase in the next few years.

Following Directions: How It Works

Directions describe how to do something. You follow one or more steps to complete the directions.

Sometimes, written directions can be hard to follow. Here's one strategy that can help you understand written directions.

1. Read the directions all the way through.

Read all of the directions. Study all visual information—such as diagrams—that come with them.

Find out the things that you don't know. Look up words in the dictionary. Use your reading skills to help you figure out passages. For example, look for what to do (the cause) in order to make something happen (the effect). Or ask someone for help.

2. Define the final result.

Ask yourself, "What are the directions for? What will I accomplish by doing all the steps?"

3. Think out each step that you must follow.

Read the directions again. In your mind, see yourself doing each step. Write the steps in your own words to make a guide.

4. Do the steps.

As you complete each step, check it off on your guide.

5. Check your work.

When you finish all the steps, check the final result. Is it what you're supposed to have? If not, look over your outline and the directions again. Find out where you went wrong and fix it.

On this page is an example of instructions from a pesticide (PEHS-tih-seyed) product. They are directions that a nursery worker might read. Read the directions. Do step 1 of the strategy.

> *Instructions for use:* **Measure 1 teaspoon of** *Bug Killer.* **Mix 1 teaspoon of** *Bug Killer* **liquid with 1 gallon of water. Shake the mixture well. Spray on the top and bottom of plant leaves.**

What are the directions for? What should you have accomplished once you have completed all the steps?

The directions are for using a pesticide called Bug Killer *After following the steps, you should have applied* Bug Killer *to a plant.*

Look at the directions again. How many steps would you follow? What are the steps?

You would follow three steps. The first step is measuring the pesticide. The second step is mixing the pesticide with water. The third step is spraying it on the plants.

Nurseries and garden centers often sell vegetable starters. These are plants ready to be planted in a customer's garden. Nursery workers make vegetable starters from a package of seeds. They follow the directions on the seed packages.

Here's an example of directions that nursery workers might read. Read the directions. Then, answer the questions on the next page.

seedlings (SEED-lihngz) tiny new plants grown from seeds

transplant (TRANS-plant) to dig up a plant and put it in another place to grow

sow to plant seeds in soil

germinate (JER-muh-nayt) to begin to grow

McDavid's Seeds **BIG RED TOMATOES**
Huge, juicy, red tomatoes

(Unused seeds good for 3 years)

For best results, start tomato **seedlings** indoors.
Start the seedlings 6 to 8 weeks before you want to **transplant** them outdoors.

Directions:

1. Put potting soil into a large pot. **Sow** the seeds 1/4 inch deep in the pot. The seeds should be about 2 inches apart. Press the seeds lightly into the soil. Then cover the seeds with more soil. Gently sprinkle water over the soil.

2. Keep the soil moist at all times. (Don't overwater the soil so that it is muddy.) The soil should stay warm at all times. It should be between 70 and 80 degrees. If conditions are right, the seeds will take 7 to 10 days to **germinate**.

3. When the seedlings have two to three sets of leaves, transplant each seedling to a 4-inch pot. Follow directions carefully for the potting soil that you use.

4. When night temperatures stay above 55 degrees, begin giving the seedlings sunlight. On the first day, put the seedlings in the sun for a few hours. Each day, let the seedlings stay out longer in the sun. By the end of the week, the seedlings should be in the sun for a whole day. This prepares the seedlings for being transplanted into the ground.

5. Transplant the seedlings to the ground on a cool or cloudy day. Make sure part of the stem of each seedling is buried. This will force more roots to grow. Water the seedlings daily until they begin to grow quickly.

Answer each question based on the directions on page 72.

1. What would be the final result of following the directions?
   a. Large, red, juicy tomatoes are ready to be eaten.
   b. Tomato seedlings are ready to be planted in a garden.
   c. Tomato seedlings have been planted in the garden.
   d. Tomato seedlings have been put out in the sun.

2. How do you start tomato seedlings?
   a. Seeds are sprinkled on the surface of the ground.
   b. Seeds are sprinkled on the surface of potting soil.
   c. Seeds are germinated in water.
   d. Seeds are sown about two inches apart in a pot of soil.

3. When do you transplant seedlings into their own 4-inch pot?
   a. After 7–10 days, transplant seedlings into pots.
   b. When nights are over 70 degrees, transplant seedlings into pots.
   c. When two to three sets of leaves appear, transplant seedlings into pots.
   d. When the first seedling has four leaves, transplant all seedlings into a pot.

4. When do you start putting the seedlings in the sun?
   a. After the first leaf appears on a seedling, put it in the sun.
   b. You can put the seedlings in the sun after 10 days.
   c. Once the seeds have germinated, the plants can go in the sun.
   d. Put seedlings out in the sun when nights stay above 55 degrees.

5. Put these steps in order. Write _1_ for the first step, _2_ for the second step, and so on.
   ___ a. Sow the tomato seeds in a pot of soil.
   ___ b. Prepare a pot of soil for sowing the tomato seeds.
   ___ c. Put the seedlings out in the sun when night temperatures are warm enough.
   ___ d. Transplant the seedlings to a 4-inch pot when two or three sets of leaves appear on them.

Check your answers on page 118.

Paul is a nursery worker. He works in a large garden center that has its own greenhouses. He was hired a few weeks ago.

This is his first job working in a garden center. He has worked in other agricultural (ag-rih-KUHL-chuhr-uhl) jobs. As a teenager, he worked in orchards and vegetable fields during the summers. He picked pears and apples. He hoed weeds in tomato fields. He helped water fields of corn and sugar beets. His first full-time job was working for a gardener.

At the garden center, Paul does mostly physical work. He unloads new shipments of soil, plants, pots, and so on. He loads heavy bags and plants into customers' cars. He puts plants out on the display tables. He waters plants and sprays them to control bugs.

The other day, Paul's supervisor heard Paul talk to a customer about planting peppers. Afterwards, the supervisor said, "Paul, tomorrow, you'll work in the greenhouse. You can start seedlings."

"All right," Paul said excitedly. This was the kind of work he wanted to do. Paul liked growing things. His own room was full of houseplants. It was like a jungle. And every year he would start a vegetable garden for his grandmother.

His grandparents used to be vegetable farmers. His grandmother once said to Paul, "You've got a green thumb, Pauly. Just like your grandfather. You ever want to start a vegetable farm, I'll put up the money."

Paul thought having a farm would be too much for him to handle. But he liked working in the garden center. Maybe, he thought, he could start his own nursery. But that would be years from now. He still had a lot to learn.

TALK ABOUT IT

1. Describe two materials that Paul might read on his job.

2. What subjects could Paul read about to help him learn more about owning a nursery?

Nursery workers sometimes transplant houseplants into bigger pots. They use different kinds of **potting soil.** They read the package labels to find which kind to use. They also read the labels for directions on how to use potting soils.

On this page is an example of a package label that nursery workers might read. Read the label. Then, answer the questions on the next page.

R•E•A•D•Y T•O U•S•E•!
FARMER DICK'S HOUSEPLANT POTTING SOIL

FARMER DICK'S HOUSEPLANT POTTING SOIL is balanced with all the essential nutrients for your plants. It's recommended for all houseplants. You can use it for ferns, palms, ivies, and philodendrons. Also, use it for spider plants, ti plants, rubber plant trees, and ficus. It's good for flowering houseplants, such as gardenias, fuschias, and violets, too.

Farmer Dick's contains only natural ingredients. It is a balanced blend of perlite, peat moss, charcoal, and forest products.

Directions for transplanting all houseplants with

FARMER DICK'S HOUSEPLANT POTTING SOIL

- Fill the new container half-way with FARMER DICK'S HOUSEPLANT POTTING SOIL.

- Remove your house plant from its old container. Brush away any extra soil from its roots. Set the plant aside.

- Set your plant into the new container. Gently press the potting soil around the roots of the plant.

- Fill the container with more potting soil. Fill it up until the soil is a half-inch from the top edge of the container.

- Water your plant thoroughly.

- Place your plant in a cool, sunless spot. After a few days, return it to its usual resting spot.

Note: Your houseplant should be moist when transplanting it. If the plant is dry, first soak it overnight. Then transplant it the next day.

Answer each question based on the label on page 75.

1. What is the product?

The product is a

2. What is the product used for?

The product is used for

3. You must follow six steps to complete the directions. In the correct order, and in your own words, write the steps below. The first one is done for you.

a. *Step 1*: Fill half of the new container with potting soil.

b. *Step 2*:

c. *Step 3*:

d. *Step 4*:

e. *Step 5*:

f. *Step 6*:

Check your answers on page 118.

◆ LESSON WRAP-UP

In this lesson, you learned that directions are a set of instructions. They describe the steps that you follow for doing something. You learned a strategy that can help you understand written directions The steps are:

1. Read the directions completely through. Look up any words that you don't know. Figure out sentences that don't make sense.
2. Describe the result you should have after the steps are completed.
3. Read the directions again, seeing each step as you read it. Write the steps in your own words to make a guide.
4. Do each step, checking it off on your guide.
5. Check your work.

Workers read many different sets of directions. Some directions may be for operating machines. Other directions may explain how to do a task. It's important that workers understand directions. They need to follow any set of directions safely and correctly.

1. Think about materials that you read at home, at work, and in school. How would using a strategy help you follow written directions?

Finish the sentence below.

Using a strategy can help me follow written directions because

2. Think about a set of directions that you have read on a job. What was the job? What did you read? Why was it important that you could follow the written directions?

Write a paragraph based on the questions above.

Check your answers on page 118.

1. Write a strategy for reading and understanding a diagram.

2. Explain the relationship between a cause and an effect.

3. Write a strategy for following directions correctly.

4. You learned about some horticulture jobs. Which job are you interested in doing or learning more about? Why are you interested in this job? How could you learn more about it? Why would it be important for you to have strong reading skills for this job?

Write a paragraph based on these questions.

Check your answers on page 118.

· Jobs in Gardening ·

Gardening jobs are part of the horticulture industry. Horticulture is the science of growing plants. You can find gardening jobs with the government or with private companies. You can also find jobs with gardening services that work mainly for home owners. Most gardening jobs involve planting and caring for trees, flowers, shrubs, and other garden plants. Some gardening jobs require only a certain type of work such as lawn care or pest control.

Garden workers read many kinds of materials. They might read charts and visual information to help them solve problems. They might read fliers about gardening products to learn more about them. They might read gardening magazines to learn new or better ways to do a job. You will learn about some of these materials in this unit.

This unit teaches the following reading skills:

◆ understanding visual information
◆ distinguishing facts from opinions
◆ drawing conclusions

You will learn how garden workers use these reading skills in their work.

Working as a Groundskeeper

Words to Know

blades

carburetor

defective

muffler

spring

You are mowing the lawn. The lawn mower makes an awful noise. It stops. It won't start again. What should you do?

In the workplace, problems with machines sometimes happen. For groundskeepers, those machines may be lawn mowers. Sometimes, a groundskeeper can figure out and fix what's wrong with a machine. That's called *trouble-shooting*. In this lesson, you'll read materials that workers use for trouble-shooting when they have problems with machines.

Operating manuals are materials that workers might read. These manuals describe the parts of a machine. They also describe how to keep a machine working. Most operating manuals have a trouble-shooting chart. It describes problems that may happen to a machine.

A chart is a kind of visual information. Reading a chart is an important skill for workers who read manuals and use machines. In this lesson, you'll learn how to **understand visual information** in charts.

Job Focus

The job of a **groundskeeper** also goes by these names: garden worker, park worker, and caretaker. A groundskeeper might work for the government—city, state, and federal—taking care of parks, school grounds, and gardens. A groundskeeper might also work for companies, business parks, and sports stadiums.

Groundskeepers do many kinds of tasks. They plant lawns, shrubs, flowers, and other plants. They also take care of plants and lawns. A groundskeeper should be able to do minor repairs of tools, machines, and other equipment.

The U.S. government reports that groundskeeping is one of the fastest-growing jobs.

Understanding Visual Information: How It Works

A **trouble-shooting chart** helps workers solve common problems that might happen to a machine.

Trouble-shooting charts show cause-and-effect relationships. The details are in two columns. One column lists the problems that might happen to a machine (effects). The other column lists possible reasons for a problem happening (causes). One or more reasons may be listed for a problem.

Here's how to read a trouble-shooting chart:

1. Find the problem on the trouble-shooting chart. Find the column that lists the problems. The headings for this column may be something like *Problem* or *What's Wrong?*

Read down the column until you find the problem that describes what is happening to your machine.

2. Read each cause. Then, check it out on your machine. Once you've found the problem, go across to the other column. That column may have a heading like *Possible Causes*. Causes are listed in the order that they should be checked on a machine. First, read a cause; then, see if that is the reason for the problem.

On this page is an example of a trouble-shooting chart. It's for a hedge trimmer. It is a chart that a groundskeeper might read. Read the chart.

Problem	Possible Causes
The **engine** does not start.	❑ The machine may be out of gas. Check gas tank. ❑ The machine may not have enough oil. Check oil level.

Which column lists the problems? Which column lists the causes for the problems?

_____

The *left* column lists the problems. The *right* column lists the possible causes for the problems.

A groundskeeper's hedge trimmer won't start. Find this problem on the chart. What are the possible reasons for this problem?_____

The chart shows two reasons: *The machine may need more gas or more oil.*

What should you check first in the hedge trimmer?

_____

You should do this first: *See if there's any gas in the gas tank.*

On their jobs, groundskeepers use many machines, such as lawn mowers. They use the operating manuals to help them handle their machines. Most of the operating manuals have trouble-shooting charts. On this page is part of a trouble-shooting chart for a lawn mower. Read the trouble-shooting chart.

carburetor
(KAHR-buh-ray-tuhr) the part of an engine in which fuel is mixed with air

blades the cutting parts of a cutting machine

defective (dih-FEHK-tihv) broken

muffler (MUF-luhr) a device that keeps an engine quiet

TROUBLE-SHOOTING YOUR LAWN MOWER

What's Wrong?	What to Check
The lawn mower is hard to start.	❑ Check the **carburetor**. It may be dirty or plugged up. ❑ Check the vent on the gas tank. It may be plugged up. ❑ Check the gas line. Fuel may not be reaching the engine.
The lawn mower does not start.	❑ Check the **blades**. They may have grass clippings stuck on them or string wrapped around them. ❑ Check the blades. They may be damaged. ❑ Check the starter. It may be **defective**. ❑ Check the engine. It may be defective.
The lawn mower lacks power.	❑ Check the gas tank. The wrong fuel may have been used. (Use only unleaded fuel.) ❑ Check the air cleaner. It may be plugged up. ❑ Check the **muffler.** It may be plugged up.

Answer each question based on the chart on page 82.

1. Which of these things is *not* on the trouble-shooting chart?
    a. the parts to check for trouble
    b. different causes for a problem
    c. problems with a machine
    d. how to fix each problem

2. Which of these problems does the trouble-shooting chart give possible causes for? (More than one problem can be chosen.)
    a. A lawn mower lacks power.
    b. A lawn mower does not start.
    c. A lawn mower jumps forward when it starts up.
    d. A lawn mower gets too hot.

3. If a lawn mower lacks power, what should you check?
    a. Check the air cleaner to see if it's plugged up.
    b. Check the carburetor to see if it's dirty.
    c. Check the blades to see if they are damaged.
    d. Check the spark plug to see if it's plugged up.

4. Suppose the lawn mower is hard to start. The carburetor is O.K. What else could be wrong?
    a. The air cleaner is plugged up.
    b. Fuel is not getting to the engine.
    c. The engine may be defective.
    d. The engine does not have enough power.

5. If you put the wrong fuel in a lawn mower, what could happen?
    a. The engine might not start.
    b. The engine might not have enough power.
    c. The engine might get ruined.
    d. The engine might get too hot.

6. If the lawn mower doesn't start, what should you check first?
    a. Check the blades for damage.
    b. Check the starter for a defective part.
    c. Check the engine for a defective part.
    d. Check the blades for something stuck on or wrapped around them.

Check your answers on page 118.

Tia works for the City Parks. She's a groundskeeper. She is part of Mr. Smith's crew. Mr. Smith is her supervisor (SOO-puhr-veyez-uhr).

The park groundskeepers do hard, physical work. They worked especially hard these last few weeks. A storm passed through. It made an awful mess in all of the 15 city parks. Trees needed to be cleared off paths. Damaged trees had to be trimmed or completely cut down. Branches had to be sawed into logs.

Mr. Smith was impressed with the way Tia worked. He noticed how she worked skillfully and safely. For two days, Tia had to handle logs that weighed 50 pounds or more.

"This is a piece of cake," she told him. "I'm the oldest in my family. I had four younger brothers and sisters to carry."

Mr. Smith likes the way Tia asks questions and listens to the answers. She takes notes a lot. When he gives her tasks to do, she writes them in a small notebook. He has seen her pull it out and check off the tasks as she finishes them.

He's also happy that Tia is good with machines. She's one of two crew members that can fix machines. Mr. Smith gave her trouble-shooting charts from the machine operating manuals. Tia reads them to figure out what's wrong with some of the machines. The other day she was able to repair an old chain saw when it was really needed. Mr. Smith even gave Tia charts showing which parts of power mowers and trimmers wear out. Tia reads the charts to decide what spare parts should be ordered for the machines.

Today, Mr. Smith will tell Tia to work at Martin Luther King, Jr. Park. She'll be part of the team that plants a new lawn. They'll also plant rose bushes and trim some overgrown hedges.

TALK ABOUT IT

1. Describe two materials that Tia might read on her job.

2. Discuss gardening subjects that Tia might read about on her own. How would the subjects be useful for her at work?

A string trimmer is another machine that groundskeepers use on their jobs. This machine is used for cutting weeds. Most operating manuals for string trimmers have a trouble-shooting chart.

On this page is part of a trouble-shooting chart for a gas-powered string trimmer. Read the trouble-shooting chart. Then, answer the questions.

STRING TRIMMER TROUBLE-SHOOTING	
What's the Problem?	Possible Causes
The engine starts up, then dies right away.	The carburetor may be plugged up with dirt.
The engine starts up more slowly than usual.	1. Trash may be wrapped around the blades. 2. Mud may be stuck on the blades. 3. The blades may be too dull.
The engine gets too hot.	1. The engine may be overworked by very heavy weeds. 2. The engine fan may be dirty or plugged up.
A white smoke comes out of the engine and gas can be smelled.	The engine may have too much fuel in it.
After pulling the rope to start the engine, the rope doesn't slide back in.	The **spring** may be broken.

spring a part that returns to its original shape after being held out of shape

Anwer each question based on the trouble-shooting chart on page 85.

1. What's one reason that a string trimmer might start up more slowly than usual?

2. If you put too much fuel in a string trimmer, what might happen?

3. Suppose the engine on a string trimmer is running, but the starter rope just hangs there. What probably happened?

4. Suppose you start the engine on a string trimmer. It stays on for a few seconds and then stops. It does this three times. What part of the machine should you check? Why?

5. Before using a string trimmer, check its blades. They should be sharp and free of mud or trash. Why is this a good idea?

6. If the engine on a string trimmer gets too hot, you should stop the machine right away. Two things may have caused it to get too hot. What are they? Write them in the order that you should check them.

   a. Check first:

   b. Check second:

Check your answers on page 118.

◆ LESSON WRAP-UP

In this lesson, you learned how to get information from a trouble-shooting chart. This special chart is one kind of visual information. You would find it in most operating manuals for machines, such as a lawn mower.

A trouble-shooting chart lists common problems that might happen to a machine. For each problem, it lists possible causes. The chart usually lists the causes in the order that they should be checked. To get information from a trouble-shooting chart, you might do these steps:

1. Find the problem on the trouble-shooting chart.
2. Read each cause. Then, check it out on your machine.

Trouble-shooting charts are some of the materials that workers read on the job. You can see how important it is for workers to understand information in charts. They help workers find out what may be wrong with a machine that they use on the job.

1. Think about the materials that you read at home, at work, and in school. How will it help improve your reading if you can read trouble-shooting charts?

Finish the sentence below.

Reading trouble-shooting charts can improve my reading because

2. Think about a job that you have had or that you have now. When might you need a chart for information? Why would it be important for you to understand that chart on your job?

Write a paragraph based on the questions above.

Check your answers on page 119.

Working in Pest Control

▼▼▼▼▼▼▼▼▼▼▼▼

Words to Know

chassis

exterminator

horticulture

ingredients

insecticide

penetrates

residue

toxins

valve

Suppose you are at work. Your boss is not happy with a product your company uses. She is looking for new products to try. She left you this note:

> Read the information on this new pesticide. What's it made of? Is it worth buying? Is it better than the brand we have now? Tell me what you think.

The note asks you to *review*, or study, a product. It asks you to decide what you think of the product. It might work better than what you use now. Or it might not.

In this lesson, you'll read materials that are related to reviewing products on the job. When reading about products, workers must **distinguish facts from opinions**. This means knowing the difference between facts and opinions. That helps workers understand what they're reading. It also helps workers make decisions about the products they review.

Job Focus

The job of **pest control assistant** might also be called a pest control technician, pest controller, or scout.

A pest control assistant helps in controlling insects, rodents, weeds, and other pests. He or she might control pests in agricultural fields, buildings, and homes.

A pest control assistant may do any of these tasks: setting up traps, spraying buildings and fields for insects, spraying or burning weeds, and finding the nests and homes of pests. He or she must be able to identify different kinds of pests. He or she must also understand how the different pests behave.

Because of growth in agriculture, jobs for pest control assistants should increase.

Distinguishing Facts from Opinions: How It Works

Authors usually use both facts and opinions in a piece of writing. This is the difference:

Facts are statements that can be proven true. "It's raining outside" is a fact. You can look outside and see whether it's raining or not.

Opinions are someone's beliefs or views about something. A writer might state how good something looks—pretty, ugly, heavy, beautiful, and so on. "A rainy day is beautiful" is an opinion. You might think rain is ugly.

In an ad, you will often find opinions. A company's ad might say, "We offer the best service." Or the ad says the company has the best product. An ad will also give you facts. For example, a fact might be, "We offer 24-hour service."

On this page is an ad for a pest control company. You might see this ad in the yellow pages of a phone book. Read the ad.

Which of the following is a fact? _____

   a. The company has a license.
   b. The company has the safest workers.

The answer is a. This statement can be proven. You could call the proper government office to find out about the company's license.

The other statement is not a fact. People would have different opinions about what makes the "safest workers."

Which of the following details is an opinion?

a. The company uses materials that meet government standards.

b. The company has the fastest service in the area.

The answer is b. Some people may believe this company is the fastest. Other people may not think so.

Pest control assistants might read reviews about new products. A *product review* is a kind of article. The author writes about a product that he or she has studied closely.

On this page is an example of a product review that a pest control assistant might find in a gardening magazine. Read the product review.

chassis (CHAS-ee) a frame that something moves back and forth on

valve the part of a pipe that allows a liquid, such as water, to flow through it

exterminator (ehk-STER-mih-nayt-uhr) a person who gets rid of pests completely

---

BEST PEST SPRAYER
NEW FROM BUGS, INC.

New on the Market

Do you have large spraying jobs that you need to get done? Do you want a sprayer that's easy to handle? Then, the best choice for you is the new *Best Pest Sprayer.*

Pest controllers have been asking for a design like *Best Pest Sprayer* for years. It has a 10-gallon tank. The tank sits on a **chassis** with 12-inch tires. It has these features:

- A 12-volt battery does the pumping for you.
- A 10-foot hose lets you spray up to 40 feet.
- A shut-off **valve** on the tank lets you seal it off. You can clean parts without draining the tank.

What do customers think? Here's what Don Johnson, owner of Vice Pest Control, has to say: "The *Best Pest Sprayer* gives me a powerful and even spray. I like the fact that I can pull it behind me, especially when I need to cover a lot of ground."

Pest **exterminator** Verna Johnson writes, "It is awkward and heavy when it's full. But that's ok. I'm not carrying it. I can always depend on the *Best Pest Sprayer* doing a good job for me."

Bugs, Inc., is one of a few companies that tests products with people who will be using them day in and day out. The *Best Pest Sprayer* is the result of five years of customer surveys and tests. Actual pest controllers tested all earlier designs.

Answer each question based on the selection on page 90. Read each statement. If you think it is a fact, underline Fact. If you think it is an opinion, underline Opinion. Then, explain your answer.

Example

Fact <u>Opinion</u>   The *Best Pest Sprayer* is easy to use.

This is an opinion because it can't be proven. Some people may not think it is easy to use.

Fact Opinion   1. The *Best Pest Sprayer* rolls on wheels.

Fact Opinion   2. The *Best Pest Sprayer* cleans quickly.

Fact Opinion   3. The *Best Pest Sprayer* is awkward to handle.

Fact Opinion   4. The *Best Pest Sprayer* sprays a long distance.

Fact Opinion   5. Pest control technicians tested earlier designs of the *Best Pest Sprayer*.

Fact Opinion   6. Don Johnson gave an opinion about the *Best Pest Sprayer* for the product review.

Check your answers on page 119.

Crawling beneath the house, Nick was glad he was short and thin. He couldn't imagine his boss, Pete, getting through this narrow space. Pete was too thick around the waist.

"You find anything?" Pete called from the outside of the house.

"Not yet," Nick called back.

Nick aimed his flashlight along the wooden frame. There were signs of termites. The owner should spray for pests. But he'd most likely decide to wait. Yeah, he'll wait until it's too late, thought Nick.

The pest control assistant worked his way toward the middle of the house. Mice were what Nick was looking for. Soon, he could hear tiny feet and tiny squeaks coming from between the walls. He looked for the best places to set up traps.

Nick made his way back to the entrance. He thought about the test he was taking today. He hoped he had studied enough. If he passed, he would have his license to be a pest exterminator.

His girlfriend didn't think much of his job. "You could do anything, Nick." Well, this was what he *wanted* to do. The job was more than killing bugs. It was more like being a bug private eye. You had to find the little creatures, figure out what they were, and then decide on the best way to get rid of them.

He learned a lot about his job from Pete. But he learned a lot more from books and magazines.

As Nick neared the entrance, he wondered if Pete meant what he had said one day. "Nick, if you still like being an exterminator in three years, we'll talk about your becoming a partner."

There's a lot of good, honest money in pest control, Nick thought. Most people need an exterminator once in a while.

1. Why should Nick understand the difference between fact and opinion in his job?

2. Why should Nick read books and magazines on pest control?

Often, companies write about their products. They send out the information to customers in different forms. One form might be a flier.

Here's an example of a flier that pest control assistants might read on their job. Read the flier.

---

insecticide
(ihn-SEHK-tih-seyed) product that is used to kill bugs

penetrates
(PEHN-ih-trayts) passes into something

ingredients
(ihn-GREE-dee-uhnts) things combined together to form a mixture

toxins (TAHK-sihnz) poisons

horticulture
(HAWR-tih-kuhl-chuhr) the science of growing plants

residue (REHZ-ih-doo) what remains after a liquid has dried

INTRODUCING
NATURAL BUG KILLER

The Nature Ways Company is happy to announce a brand-new **insecticide—Natural Bug Killer**. It's another great product that is safe for people, plants, and the land.

Natural Bug Killer is a petroleum-free insecticide. It can be used on almost all plants. It's safe for peaches, kiwi fruit, strawberries, and other fruit plants. It's safe for beans, squash, tomatoes, and almost all vegetable plants. And it's safe for the lawn and garden plants, such as flowers, shrubs, and trees.

Natural Bug Killer **penetrates** the cell membranes of soft-bodied insects. It attacks their nervous systems instantly. Customers will find that it easily controls:

- aphids, beetles, and chinch bugs
- caterpillars and larvae
- white flies and leafhoppers

This product contains only natural **ingredients.** The ingredients will decompose and provide essential nutrients for your soil.

Toxins in the insecticide begin breaking down within 24 hours after applying it.

Natural Bug Killer is easy to use. Shake the bottle. Add one part to 20 parts of water. Then, spray your plants.

Dr. J. Williams-Singh, **horticulture** professor at University of Lisbon, highly recommends this new product. "We have **Natural Bug Killer** on our experimental plants. We find it safe to use. It breaks down completely. It leaves no **residue** on the plants or in the soil. In fact, it adds essential nutrients to the soil."

Nature Ways Company is sure you will be satisfied with this product, or we will refund your money in full.

These facts are based on the selection on page 93. Read each fact. Then, make up an opinion based on that fact.

Example

Fact: Nature Ways, Inc., makes *Natural Bug Killer*.

Opinion: Nature Ways, Inc., makes only the best natural insecticides.

1. Fact: *Natural Bug Killer* is an insecticide.
    Opinion: Natural Bug Killer

2. Fact: *Natural Bug Killer* has only natural ingredients.
    Opinion: The ingredients

3. Fact: The toxins in *Natural Bug Killer* break down into the soil.
    Opinion: Toxins

4. Fact: Insects get *Natural Bug Killer* into their systems and die from it.
    Opinion: Insects

5. Fact: One part *Natural Bug Killer* is added to 20 parts water to make a spray.
    Opinion: Making *Natural Bug Killer* solution

6. Fact: Nature Ways Company will give customers a refund if they are not satisfied with *Natural Bug Killer*.
    Opinion: Customers

Check your answers on page 119.

In this lesson, you learned how to tell facts from opinions in a piece of writing. A fact is something that can be proven to be true. An opinion is someone's belief or view.

It is important for workers to be able to tell facts from opinions. You've seen how important it is in reading ads and product reviews in this lesson. Workers also need to tell the difference between facts and opinions in office memos, work reports, job procedures, and other work materials. Noting statements that are facts and opinions is helpful to understanding any written material.

1. Think about the materials that you read at home, at work, and in school. How will it help improve your reading if you can tell the difference between facts and opinions?

Finish the sentence below.

Identifying facts and opinions can improve my reading because

2. Think about a job for which you had to read materials with both facts and opinions. What was the job? What did you read? Why was it important to identify facts and opinions in your reading?

Write a paragraph based on the questions above.

Check your answers on page 119.

Caring for Plants and Lawns

cultivating

decompose

dense

organic

The gardening section of a newspaper is one type of material that gardeners might read. Books and magazines are others. So are information sheets and fliers that gardening shops might give out for free.

Gardeners often read to learn more about plants. They may read about specific plants, such as roses. They read materials about new or improved gardening methods, tools, and products. In this lesson, you'll read materials about taking care of plants and lawns.

Workers use the information they read to help them understand something in a new way. They use the information to **draw a conclusion.**

Job Focus

A **gardener** might work for or own a gardening service. These gardening services are usually hired by home owners, small apartment building owners, and small companies. The services often work once a week or once a month for them.

A gardener's tasks may include creating a landscaping (LAND-skayp-ihng) plan. Landscaping is making land more pleasant to look at by arranging plants. A gardener may also set plants, mow lawns, care for yards, and apply sprays to kill insects. Gardening jobs will increase into the next century. This is because more home owners are hiring gardening services to do their landscaping.

About 300,000 workers have jobs with lawn and garden service businesses. Some of these people work for themselves. Still more gardening workers have jobs with government, cemetaries, theme parks, and garden stores.

Drawing Conclusions: How It Works

Drawing conclusions means coming to a new understanding based on information you read. Conclusions are also based on your own knowledge and experiences.

Following a strategy when you read can help you draw conclusions. Here's one that you might use.

1. Answer the following questions:
   What information have I learned from reading? What facts and details do I already know?

2. Ask yourself this question:
   Can I use the reading and what I know to answer a new question?

3. Now you are ready to draw a conclusion. Think about adding up your information in the following way:
   What I read + what I know = a new idea or understanding. Try to use your new idea to answer a question you asked in step 2.

On this page is a memo that a landscape worker might get on the job. Read the memo. Try the strategy.

HUYNH & ROSE LANDSCAPING SERVICES

To: Charlie, Tharon, Annabelle, and Freddy

We can all agree that the Ford-Grant project was a difficult one. The job would not be done without your hard work. You put in long hours and made the extra effort so we could get done on time. Ford and Grant are so pleased that they've given us a $2,000 bonus. Enjoy your share. Thank you!

What is one specific question you might draw a conclusion about? _____

Some questions that you might ask are *how do Huynh & Rose treat their employees? Would Huynh & Rose do another job for Ford-Grant? Why do you think Ford-Grant gave a bonus?*

What conclusion might you draw to this question: How do Huynh & Rose treat their employees? What details would you base your conclusion on?

_____

One conclusion you might draw is this: *The employers treat their employees well.* Some facts you could use to draw this conclusion are *they thanked them for their hard work and gave them a share of the bonus.*

Gardeners might read gardening books to learn more about their jobs. Gardening books cover many subjects about gardening. On this page is an introduction to pruning (PROON-ihng). Pruning means careful cutting to control how plants grow. Read the introduction.

Why Prune? An Introduction

Tree branches that had been damaged in a storm are cut off. Tips on a house plant are pinched off so that the plant will become fuller. These are two examples of pruning.

Pruning is a way of **cultivating** plants. Plants are cut back from the top, sides, and center. People prune shrubs, hedges, trees, house plants, and other plants for any number of reasons.

Dr. Julie Sanchez, Chairman of the Horticulture Department at Lee College, says, "Pruning is a form of housekeeping. It's how we care for plants, keeping them neat as well as pretty. For instance, when our ivy has a dry stem or dry leaves, we pluck them off. That's pruning."

Pruning is also used for keeping plants in control. We prune plants when they become too **dense**. This allows air and light to reach the inside and lower parts of the plants.

Pruning, says Dr. Sanchez, is also good medicine for plants. Dead parts of a tree or any plant should be pruned immediately. The parts may have died due to disease. Pruning keeps the disease from spreading.

Pruning also can be used to control a plant's growth. When a stem or branch that grows in a certain direction is cut, growth is stopped. New growth will begin in another direction. Pruning also lets gardeners keep plants, such as pine trees, to a certain height and width.

For those who raise fruit trees, pruning each year can produce a full crop. And with a special kind of pruning, a new or better fruit can be developed.

To prune or not to prune? Is there any reason why you shouldn't?

cultivating
(KUHL-tuh-vayt-ihng)
improving or developing plants with special methods such as pruning

dense crowded together

Answer each question based on the selection on page 98.

1. Why is pruning an important skill for gardeners to have?
   a. It's their job to mow the lawn.
   b. It's their job to clean up the yard.
   c. It's their job to maintain healthy plants.
   d. It's their job to keep plants small.

2. Why do you think Dr. Julie Sanchez is quoted in the introduction?
   a. She is an expert on plants.
   b. She is a medical doctor.
   c. She likes plants.
   d. She's a good friend of the author.

3. What is an example of pruning?
   a. A gardener plants a rose bush.
   b. A gardener sprays a rose bush for insects.
   c. A gardener snips off dead roses from the bush.
   d. A gardener gives a rose bush plant food so it will grow better.

4. Suppose you have a house plant, such as ivy. Part of it seems to be rotting. A gardener friend suggests that you prune it. Why is that a good idea?
   a. The ivy would look better without the rotting part.
   b. The rotting part of the plant may be diseased. By removing it, you may be able to save the rest of the plant.
   c. Pruning the rotting part would force new growth to grow in a different direction.
   d. The rotting part is a sign of the plant being too dense. It's not getting enough light or water.

5. Imagine that part of a hedge has been run into by a car. The gardener suggests pruning it. Why is that a good idea?
   a. It will keep disease from spreading.
   b. It will keep it from getting too big.
   c. Pruning it will allow more fruit to grow.
   d. Pruning will clean up the broken branches.

Check your answers on page 119.

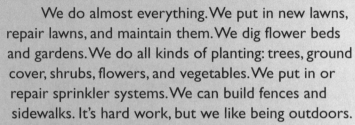

Andy and I own a gardening and lawn service. Both of us had worked as groundskeepers at the M.T. Football Stadium for years. That's where we met. When we got laid off, we decided to start our own business—Andy and Tess, Gardeners Are Us!

We do almost everything. We put in new lawns, repair lawns, and maintain them. We dig flower beds and gardens. We do all kinds of planting: trees, ground cover, shrubs, flowers, and vegetables. We put in or repair sprinkler systems. We can build fences and sidewalks. It's hard work, but we like being outdoors.

Our business has been good from the start. A lot of houses are being built in our town. Soon, it will be more like a small city.

Andy and I like to do jobs in the richer neighborhoods. That way, we have fewer, bigger jobs. Little jobs take up more time.

Andy is studying for the GED test. He won't have any problem passing it. He's good in math and reading. His spelling needs work, but he can write a good essay. Andy is proud, and he wants our customers to think he is smart—which he is, GED or no GED.

I'm taking art classes. They help me see lines and shapes and understand how colors work together. That comes in handy when you're designing landscapes.

We notice that many of our customers like to have theme gardens designed for them. Some customers change their themes every few years. We want to add that to our services. So we've both enrolled in a landscaping design program. Once we get our design certificates, we'll feel better about offering design services. Some customers like to know you have that certificate. We've got one year left to go.

TALK ABOUT IT

1. Describe two work materials that Andy and Tess might read.

2. Discuss why having the landscaping design certificates would help Andy and Tess get more business.

Once a week, most newspapers have a gardening section or column. Gardeners can learn useful or new information about gardens, lawns, and landscaping.

Here's an example of a gardening column. Read the column.

decompose
(dee-kuhm-POHZ) to rot or break down

The Gardener's Corner

A Natural Way of Caring For Lawns—Really!

It used to be that when you took care of a lawn, you used a lot of water and fertilizer. You gave it a "crew cut" and made sure all grass clippings were raked from it. You pulled weeds and applied bug killer. What was the result? Usually, a dead-looking lawn!

You can have a healthy lawn without all that hard work and without spending a lot of money. How, you ask? By caring for your lawn naturally.

The goal to natural lawn care is keeping the soil and grass roots healthy and strong. Here's what you do:

*1. Use only **organic** fertilizers.*

They release nutrients slowly, so you don't have to fertilize as much. Also, organic fertilizers break down and feed your soil.

The other thing about organic fertilizers is that they don't kill the *good* insects in your lawn. Those insects eat the bad ones—the pests that can and will eat up your lawn.

2. Mow your lawn often.

Al DeGloria, head groundskeeper at the National League Stadium, has been caring for the grounds naturally for 15 years. He says, "Keep your lawn mower blades at the highest level. You only want to clip a quarter inch off the top of your lawn each time. The grass clippings will be small and thin.

So leave them on your lawn. They'll **decompose** quickly. It's a natural fertilizer."

3. Don't overwater.

A healthy lawn means having long roots. That way your lawn can make it through the dry periods. Over-watering will create shallow roots that can't handle dry periods.

How much water should you give your lawn? During its growing season, a healthy lawn needs only an inch of water per week. David McJames, a groundskeeper, recommends soaking the lawn early in the day. He says, "I like to water in the early mornings. By the time evening comes, the grass is dry."

organic (awr-GAN-ihk) grown with the help of substances that come from plants and animals

Answer each question based on the selection on page 101. Some questions ask you to express your own opinion.

1. What's one way that natural lawn care is different from the way most people care for their lawns?

2. Do you think organic fertilizers are better than ones made from chemicals? Why?

3. Do you think people should rake grass clippings off their lawns? Why or why not?

4. Do you think that everybody should change to doing natural lawn care? Why or why not?

5. Which method would you use: the regular or natural lawn care? Why?

Check your answers on page 119.

◆ LESSON WRAP-UP

In this lesson, you learned how to draw conclusions. You saw that you can come to new understandings based on what you read. You learned this strategy to help you draw sensible conclusions:

1. Answer the questions: What have I read? What do I already know?
2. Ask the question: Can I answer a new question based on my reading and what I know?
3. Draw your conclusion by adding up what you learned to answer a new question.

As you've seen throughout the book, workers have to read many kinds of materials. For example, gardeners might read materials about caring for plants and lawns. Drawing conclusions is just one reading skill that can help workers understand and use what they read.

1. Think about the materials that you read at home, at work, and in school. How will drawing conclusions help you put your reading to good use?

Finish the sentence below.

Drawing conclusions can help me put my reading to good use because

2. Think about materials that you have read on a job. What was the job? What did you read? Why was it important to draw conclusions in order to do that job well?

Write a paragraph based on the questions above.

Check your answers on page 120.

◆ UNIT FOUR REVIEW

In this unit, you learned how to use a trouble-shooting chart. You learned about the difference between facts and opinions. And you learned a strategy for drawing conclusions from your reading.

Answer these questions about the reading skills.

1. What is a trouble-shooting chart used for?

2. How is a fact different from an opinion?

3. Why is drawing conclusions a useful reading skill?

4. In this unit, you learned about these jobs: a groundskeeper, a pest control assistant, and a private gardener. Which job are you interested in doing or learning more about? Why are you interested in this job? How could you learn more about it? Why would it be important for you to have strong reading skills for this job?

Write a paragraph based on these questions.

Check your answers on page 120.

RESPELLING GUIDE

Use the following guide to help you pronounce long and hard words.

Sound	Respelling	Example of Respelling
a as in hat	a	hat
a as in day, date, paid	ay	day, dayt, payd
vowels as in far, on, bother, hot	ah	fahr, ahn, BAH-thuhr, haht
vowels as in dare, air, heir	ai	dair, air, air
vowels as in saw, call, pore, door	aw	saw, kawl, pawr, dawr
e as in pet, debt	eh	peht, deht
e as in seat, beef, chief, **y** as in beauty	ee	seet, beef, cheef BYOO-tee
vowels as in learn, urn, fur, sir	er	lern, ern, fer, ser
i as in sit, bitter, **ee** as in been	ih	siht, BIHT-uhr, bihn
i as in mile, **ei** as in height	eye	meyel, heyet
o as in go	oh	goh
vowels as in boil, toy	oi	boil, toi
vowels as in how, out, bough	ow	how, owt, bow
vowels as in up, come	u	up, kum
vowels as in use, use, bureau, few	yoo	yooz yoose, BYOO-roh, fyoo
vowels as in look, put, foot	oo	look, poot, foot
vowels as in bitt**er**, act**io**n	uh	BIHT-uhr, AK-shuhn

Consonants are respelled as they sound. Here are a few examples.

c as in cat	k	kat
c as in dance	s	dans
ch as in Christmas	k	KRIHS-muhs
g as in gem	j	jehm
s as in laser	z	LAY-zuhr
ph as in phone	f	fohn

RESOURCES

The following organizations and publications may provide more information about the jobs covered in this book.

**United States Government
U.S. Department of Labor, Employment and Training Administration**

Adult Training Programs include the following:
Job Training Partnership Act (JTPA)
This program provides job training for disadvantaged adults who face significant employment barriers. For more information, write:

> Office of Employment and Training
> Programs, Room N4469
> U.S. Department of Labor
> 200 Constitution Ave, N.W.
> Washington, DC 20210
> ON THE INTERNET:
> http://www.doleta.gov/programs/programs.htm

Apprenticeship Training
The Bureau of Apprenticeship and Training registers apprenticeship programs in 23 states. It also assists State Apprenticeship Councils in 27 states, the District of Columbia, Puerto Rico, and the U.S. Virgin Islands. For further information, write or call:

> Bureau of Apprenticeship and Training
> U.S. Department of Labor
> 200 Constitution Ave, N.W.
> Washington, DC 20210
> PHONE (202) 219-5921
> ON THE INTERNET:
> http://www.doleta.gov/programs/programs.htm

The Bureau of Labor Statistics has descriptions of working conditions for a wide variety of specific occupational areas. For more information on the Bureau's publications, write to:

> Bureau of Labor Statistics
> Division of Information Services
> 2 Massachusetts Avenue, N.E.
> Room 2860
> Washington, DC 20212

Information specialists provide a variety of services by telephone: (202)606-5886
To send a question by fax, please call (202)606-7890
ON THE INTERNET: http://stats.bls.gov

Unit I JOBS IN FARMING

American Farm Bureau Federation
225 Touhy Avenue
Park Ridge, IL 60068
PHONE: (312) 399-5700
FAX: (312) 399-5896
ON THE INTERNET: http://www.fb.com

Washington Office
600 Maryland Avenue SW, Suite 800
Washington, DC 20024
PHONE: (202) 484-3600
FAX: (202) 484-3604

American Society of Farm Managers
950 S. Cherry Street, Suite 508
Denver, CO 80222
PHONE: (303) 758-3513

American SMALL FARM Magazine
21822 Sherman Way, Suite 200
Canoga Park, CA 91303
PHONE: (818) 716-3131
FAX: (818) 716-3171
ON THE INTERNET:
http://www.smallfarm.com/

Unit 2 JOBS WORKING WITH ANIMALS

National Dog Groomers Association of America
P. O. Box 101
Clark, PA 16113

Pet Industry Joint Advisory Council
1220 19th Street NW, Suite 400
Washington, DC 20036
PHONE: (202)452-1525
FAX: (202)293-4377

The Humane Society of the United States
Attention: Animal Caretakers Information
2100 L Street, NW
Washington, DC 20037
PHONE: (202) 452-1100
ON THE INTERNET: http://www.hsus.org

The American Association of Zoo Keepers (AAZK)
Topeka Zoological Park
635 S.W. Gage Boulevard
Topeka, KS 66606-2066
PHONE/FAX: (913) 273-1980
ON THE INTERNET: http://aazk.ind.net/

Unit 3 JOBS WORKING WITH PLANTS

Ohio Florists' Association
2130 Stella Court, Suite 200
Columbus, OH 43215-1033
PHONE: (614) 487-1117
FAX: (614) 487-1216
ON THE INTERNET: http://www.ofa.org

Greenhouse Business
The News Magazine of Profitable Growing
6300 N. River Road, Suite 505
Rosemont, IL 60018
PHONE: (847) 823-5650
FAX: (847) 696-3445

The Horticultural Web
ON THE INTERNET:
http://www.horticulture.com/

Rittners School of Floral Design
345 Marlborough St.
Boston, MA 02115
PHONE: (617) 267-3824

Nursery Technology Program
Anoka-Hennepin Technical College
PHONE: (800) 247-5588

Unit 4 JOBS IN GARDENING

Professional Lawn Care Association of America
1000 Johnson Ferry Rd., NE
C135
Marietta, GA 30068-2112
PHONE: (800) 458-3466

Professional Grounds Management Society
120 Cockeysville Rd., Suite 104
Hunt Valley, MD 21031

North American Equipment Dealers Association
10877 Watson Rd.
St. Louis, MO 63127

Associated Landscape Contractors of America, Inc.
12200 Sunrise Valley Dr., Suite 150
Reston, VA 22091

National Landscape Association
1250 I Street, NW, Suite 500
Washington, DC 20005

Reference Book
Dell, Owen E., How To Operate and Open a Home-Based Landscaping Business. Old Saybrook, CT: Globe Pequot Press, 1994.

GLOSSARY

absorb to take in a substance, such as when a sponge absorbs water

agriculture farming

association a group of people or businesses that share some interests

blades the cutting parts of a cutting machine

boarders pets that get meals and a place to stay while their owners are away from home

bountiful a lot

browse to look around

carburetor the part of an engine in which fuel is mixed with air

chassis a frame that something moves back and forth on

chemicals substances made by combining simpler elements

chlorophyll the green coloring of plants, which plants use to make carbohydrates

complimentary offered by a store or business at no charge

crop rotation to grow different crops in the same field over a four- or five-year period

cultivating improving or developing plants with special methods such as pruning

customers people who buy things from a store or business

decompose to rot or break down

defective broken

dense crowded together

digestion the body's process for breaking down food to get nutrients

display a showing or presentation of items

docked reduced

domestic bred for human use, such as for food or work

efficient doing something well with the least amount of time and work

employees people who are hired to do work for a company or business

erosion a loss of dirt caused by wind or water

exterminator a person who gets rid of pests completely

fertilization the joining of a male cell and female cell to create a new living thing

fertilizers plant foods that are added to the soil to help crops grow

flock a group of animals that live, feed, or move together

fumigate to kill insects with a gas or smoke

germinate to begin to grow

haggle to bargain or argue over prices

horticulture the science of growing plants

Human Resources the department in a company that keeps all employee records, such as records of sick leave

ingredients things combined together to form a mixture

insecticide product that is used to kill bugs

maintenance work that must be done regularly, such as cleaning

manual a book of instructions for employees

mate to join with a partner to produce and raise offspring

memorandum a short note or reminder

memo short for *memorandum*

muffler a device that keeps an engine quiet

nutrients substances that the body needs to stay healthy

organic grown with the help of substances that come from plants and animals

origin the place where something or someone came from

penetrates passes into something

pesticides substances used to kill bugs and weeds

pests weeds, bugs, or animals, such as mice or deer, that can harm crops

photosynthesis the process by which green plants use light energy to make their own food

pollen the male cells of a flower, which look like very fine, yellow dust

pollinate to put pollen on a flower to enable reproduction

potting soil a special mixture of soil used for plants grown in pots

precautions safety measures

procedure a series of steps to follow in order

quality how good something is

refund money returned to a customer

residue what remains after a liquid has dried

seedlings tiny new plants grown from seeds

soil the dark, rich top layer of dirt that plants grow in

soluble able to be dissolved

sow to plant seeds in soil

spring a part that returns to its original shape after being bent out of shape

substitute someone who is taking the place of another

supervisor someone in charge of other workers

sustainable farming a way of farming that does not harm the land

toxins poisons

transplant to dig up a plant and put it in another place to grow

valve the part of a pipe that allows a liquid, such as water, to flow through it

withers the part between the shoulder blades on a horse's back

INDEX

A N S W E R S

Unit One: Jobs in Produce Farming

Lesson 1: Working Safely in Farming

CHECK YOUR UNDERSTANDING

page 5

   1. b

   2. a

   3. a

   4. a

   5. c

CHECK YOUR UNDERSTANDING

page 8

   1. The main idea of the whole reading selection is "Follow the safety precautions when you lift objects." This is the main idea because the rest of the reading selection discusses the safety precautions.

   2. The main idea of 2. Use the right muscles is "The correct lifting muscles are your leg muscles." This is the main idea because the rest of the paragraph says why the leg muscles are the right ones to use and the back muscles are not.

   3. The main idea of 3. Lift objects properly is that it's important that you stand and bend properly when you lift objects. This is the main idea because the rest of the paragraph describes what you should do with your body as you lift things.

   4. The main idea of 5. Ask for help is "Get help when you know an object may be too hard to lift alone." This is the main idea because the rest of the paragraph describes the kind of help to get.

LESSON WRAP-UP

page 9

Here are some sample answers:

   1. Finding the main idea of a reading piece will help improve my reading because the more I practice finding the main idea, the easier it will be for me to understand harder reading selections.

   2. One summer I worked as an apricot picker. I had to read a paper about withholding taxes from my paycheck. By understanding the main idea, I could figure out how much money I wanted taken out of my paycheck.

Lesson 2: Selling at a Farmers' Market

CHECK YOUR UNDERSTANDING

page 13

   1. Here is a sample answer: To get people to buy again and again, farmers have to give good service by being polite, efficient, friendly, and enthusiastic.

   2. c, e, f, g, i

   3. Here are some sample answers:

     b. I would say hello to every customer who comes to my booth.

     c. I would thank a customer for buying some fruit.

     d. I would let customers have a taste of the pears and apples.

     e. I would have coins ready to give customers their change quickly.

CHECK YOUR UNDERSTANDING

page 16

   1. You should have underlined this sentence: To draw customers to your booth, make a neat, eye-catching display. Here is a sample answer for the reworded main idea: The main idea is farmers need to make a good-looking display that will draw customers to their booths.

   2. Here are some sample answers (they can be in any order):

     b. One supporting detail is arranging a display so that the colors of the produce appeal to the customers.

It supports the main idea because it's an

example of how to make a good-looking display.

c. One supporting detail is putting the produce at a level that customers can see and touch.

It supports the main idea because it's an example of how to make a display that will draw in customers.

d. One supporting detail is arranging the produce so that there seems to be a lot of it on the table.

It supports the main idea because it's an example of how to make a good-looking display.

LESSON WRAP-UP

page 17

Here are some sample answers:

1. Finding supporting details will help me improve my reading because it will help me find complete information and explain things such as who, when, where, how, and why.

2. I was a salesclerk at a department store. Once, I was given a memo that described new steps for checking in and checking out at work. There were a lot of details in it. If I couldn't figure out the supporting details, I might have made a mistake and upset my supervisor.

Lesson 3: Doing Research in Farming

CHECK YOUR UNDERSTANDING

page 21

1. c
2. b
3. c
4. d
5. a

6. Here is a sample answer: Farmers can try safer methods for pest control and avoid chemical pesticides.

CHECK YOUR UNDERSTANDING

Page 24

Here are some sample answers:

1. The general subject is protecting farmland.

2. The main idea of the first paragraph is that every year a lot of good farming soil is lost.

3. The main idea of the second and third paragraphs is that farmers cause a lot of soil erosion.

4. The main idea of the fourth paragraph is that farmers can cause the loss of soil quality.

5. The main idea of the last paragraph is that farmers can do certain things to protect the land.

6. The main idea of the selection is that farmers can take action to stop the loss of good soil for farming.

LESSON WRAP-UP

page 25

Answers will vary. Here are some sample answers:

1. I should figure out the main idea of the memo because if I don't fill in my time card correctly, I might get paid less than I really should.

2. I was a fast food worker. I was given a policy about absences to read. I didn't understand the policy until I asked another worker. If I had figured out the main idea, I would have understood it. Then, I could have figured out what the details were all about.

UNIT I REVIEW

page 26

1. The main idea is the most important point being made in a reading.

2. A supporting detail explains or proves something about the main idea. It tells about the who, when, where, how, or why in the reading.

3. I might figure out a main idea by finding all the details in a paragraph or paragraphs. Then I would figure out what important idea the details all support.

4. Accept all reasonable answers, such as: I would be interested in selling produce at a farmers market. I like the idea of working outside and having part-time

hours. I think it would be fun to be around a lot of people. It would be important to have good reading skills for this job because I would need to understand a lot of written things such as permits and rules.

Unit Two: Jobs Working with Animals

Lesson 4: Taking Care of Pets

CHECK YOUR UNDERSTANDING

page 31

Here are the answers, with some sample explanations:

1. a. This is correct because fleas breed in hot weather, and their bites cause animals to scratch.

2. b. This is correct because there will be poisonous fumes in the house.

3. a. This is correct because fleas are very small and could work their way back out of the vacuum cleaner bag.

4. a. This is correct because fleas come out in hot weather.

CHECK YOUR UNDERSTANDING

page 34

Here are some sample answers:

1. It might have little energy or problems with digestion.

2. A cat would get protein and fat from eating chicken.

3. No. Tuna fish would supply only some nutrients. The cat needs a wider variety of foods.

4. Yes. Chicken is a source of protein, which is needed to recover from some illnesses.

5. Yes. These foods are sources of carbohydrates, protein, and fat, as well as vitamins and minerals.

6. The cat would become dehydrated (sick from loss of fluids). It could eventually die without water.

7. No. If it's getting less exercise but the same amount of food, it will gain weight.

LESSON WRAP-UP

page 35

Here are some sample answers:

1. Making inferences can help improve my reading because it will help me find unstated ideas and get a better understanding of what I read.

2. For example: I was sales a clerk at a clothing store. Some of the things I had to read were papers about workers' benefits. Making inferences helped me figure out what the papers were talking about because not all the details were given.

Lesson 5: Working at a Zoo

CHECK YOUR UNDERSTANDING

page 39

Here are the true/false answers, with some sample explanations for those statements that are false.

1. False. The statement is false because both the donkey and the pony belong to the horse family.

2. False. The statement is false because the donkey comes from Africa, but the pony comes from Asia.

3. True

4. False. The statement is false because owners of these animals say that they are loving and friendly.

5. False. The statement is false because both animals are used for carrying heavy loads and riding.

CHECK YOUR UNDERSTANDING

page 42

Here are some sample answers:

1. Chicken and geese both have wings.

2. Chickens and geese have different feet. They also have different beaks.

3. a. Geese graze on grass for food. Chickens peck at seeds and grains for food.

   b. Geese mate for life. The rooster mates with several hens in its lifetime.

   c. Both the gander and goose take

care of their young. But only the hen takes care of young chicks.

    d. Geese and chickens act the same in a flock. They find food as a group. And there's always one bird that becomes the boss of the group.

LESSON WRAP-UP

page 43

Here are some sample answers:

    1. Comparing and contrasting details can improve my reading because it helps me understand and remember details.

    2. I was a classroom aide. I had to read test papers to make a list of students' names and their grades. I had to group students' names by the grade they got. Comparing and contrasting the details helped me do my job.

Lesson 6: Working in a Veterinary Clinic

CHECK YOUR UNDERSTANDING

page 47

    1. b
    2. b
    3. b
    4. b
    5. a
    6. b
    7. b
    8. b

CHECK YOUR UNDERSTANDING

page 50

    1. The purpose of the table is to see which workers are responsible for certain tasks each day.

    2. "Maintenance" means doing regular chores such as cleaning up.

    3. Meals and Exercise Dogs are the categories that show details for morning and afternoon.

    4. Tomas would do maintenance on Thursday if Rhon is absent.

    5. Keisha walks the dogs on Friday mornings.

    6. Mark feeds the animals on Wednesday evenings and Lynn feeds them on Thursday evenings.

    7. Weekday evening meals should be given between 6 p.m. and 7 p.m.

    8. Dr. Willits would substitute for Moses. She would give the animals their meals.

    9. a. Dr. Boyd would feed the animals.

       b. Rhon would exercise the dogs.

LESSON WRAP-UP

page 51

Here are some sample answers:

    1. Reading tables can help improve my reading because it would help me find information.

    2. I once worked at a fast food place. I had to read a daily work schedule to find out what tasks I had to do each day. If I couldn't understand the schedule, I wouldn't have been able to do the work I was supposed to do.

UNIT 2 REVIEW

page 52

    1. To make inferences you look at clues. You use clues from your own knowledge and experience of the subject. You use clues that the main idea and supporting details provide.

    2. When you compare details in a piece of writing, you're finding out how the details are alike. When you contrast details in a piece of writing, you're finding out how the details are different.

    3. To help you read a table, figure out what its purpose is and what the main details are.

    4. Accept all reasonable answers. For example: I am interested in the job of veterinarian helper. I like taking care of animals. And I think that I would like to be a veterinarian some day. It's important that I have strong reading skills for the veterinarian helper because I would be given instructions on how to do my work, when and where to do my work. I would also read a lot of books to learn about

animals. Having strong reading skills would make learning easier for me.

Unit Three: Jobs Working with Plants

Lesson 7: Working in Horticulture

CHECK YOUR UNDERSTANDING

page 57

1. c
2. a
3. c
4. c
5. a. 3
   b. 4
   c. 2
   d. 1

CHECK YOUR UNDERSTANDING

page 60

Here are some sample answers:

1. The diagram shows how a plant grows.

2. The purpose of a plant's roots is to absorb water and minerals from the soil.

3. The purpose of a plant's stem is to carry food, water, and minerals to every part of the plant.

4. a. One purpose is to make food (photosynthesis).

   b. One purpose is to take in carbon dioxide from the air and release oxygen into the air.

5. Chlorophyll in the leaves turns into food when sunlight touches the leaves.

6. If a plant doesn't get enough essential nutrients, it might not bear fruit. It will eventually wilt and die.

LESSON WRAP-UP

page 61

Here are some sample answers:

1. Reading diagrams can improve my reading because they give information about the subject in the reading.

2. I was an office clerk. I had to read a diagram of a copy machine. It was important that I understand the diagram because it showed me how to fix paper jams in the copy machine. I couldn't depend on somebody showing me how to fix the machine each time it jammed.

Lesson 8: Selling Flowers

CHECK YOUR UNDERSTANDING

page 65

1. True
2. False
3. False
4. True
5. True

6. Here is a sample answer: Businesses need these kinds of policies so that they can be fair to each customer. Otherwise, workers will not know what to do when a customer complains.

CHECK YOUR UNDERSTANDING

Page 68

Here are some sample answers:

1. A customer enters the flower shop. The assistant is not waiting on another customer.

2. The customer takes a greeting card without having to pay for it.

3. The florist will wrap the purchase with pretty greens, wrapping paper, and ribbon.

4. A customer pays for his/her purchase with a credit card.

5. Customers feel that the workers appreciate their business and are friendly.

LESSON WRAP-UP

page 69

Here are some sample answers:

1. Identifying cause and effect can improve my reading because it would help me understand what happened and what caused it.

2. I was a fast food worker. I read about the restaurant's policy on worker absences. By identifying the cause-and-effect among the details, I was able to understand what to do if I had to be absent from work.

Lesson 9: Working in a Nursery

CHECK YOUR UNDERSTANDING

page 73

   1. c

   2. d

   3. c

   4. d

   5. a. 2

     b. 1

     c. 4

     d. 3

CHECK YOUR UNDERSTANDING

page 76

Here are some sample answers:

   1. The product is a bag of potting soil.

   2. The product is used for growing house plants in containers.

   3. b. Step 2: Take the plant out of the old container and brush any extra soil from its roots.

   c. Step 3: Put the plant in the new container and cover its roots with potting soil.

   d. Step 4: Fill the rest of the container with potting soil.

   e. Step 5: Water the plant.

   f. Step 6: Place the plant in a cool area away from sunlight.

LESSON WRAP-UP

page 77

Here are some sample answers:

   1. Using a strategy can help me follow written directions because it can guide me through parts that I wouldn't understand at first.

   2. I was a gas station attendant. I had to read directions for taking off old windshield wipers and putting new ones on cars. It was important that I understand those directions because that was part of my job. If I couldn't follow the directions well, customers would be kept waiting too long.

UNIT 3 REVIEW

Page 78

   1. a. Step one: Study the diagram, reading everything on it. b. Step two: Figure out the main idea. c. Step three: Figure out the supporting details.

   2. a The cause is: Some flowers are two days old b. The effect is: Prices are marked down.

   3. a. Step 2 b. Step 5 c. Step 1 d. Step 4 e. Step 3

   4. Accept all reasonable answers. For example: I am interested in learning more about the nursery worker. I am interested in this job because I like gardening. It would be important for me to have strong reading skills as a nursery worker because I would need to know about a lot of different plants—what they are, how to plant them, whether they need sun or shade, how much to water them, and details like that.

Unit Four: Jobs in Gardening

Lesson 10: Working as a Groundskeeper

CHECK YOUR UNDERSTANDING

page 83

   1. d

   2. a, b

   3. a

   4. b

   5. b

   6. d

CHECK YOUR UNDERSTANDING

page 86

Here are some sample answers:

   1. (one of these) Trash is wrapped around the blades. Mud is stuck on the blades. The blades are dull.

   2. The engine will start to smoke and you'll smell gas.

   3. The spring broke.

   4. You should check the carburetor because it may be plugged up.

   5. If the blades are dull or wrapped in trash, the engine won't start up the way it should.

6. a. The engine is working harder than it should. That means the weeds being cut may be too much for the machine to handle.

    b. The fan on the engine may be dirty or plugged up.

LESSON WRAP-UP

page 87

Here are some sample answers:

    1. Reading trouble-shooting charts can improve my reading because I must understand cause-and-effect relationships among the details.

    2. I was a cook's helper. If something went wrong with the food blender, I could have read the trouble-shooting chart in its manual. Showing that I could understand this chart would have showed my boss that I was a problem-solver.

Lesson 11: Working in Pest Control

CHECK YOUR UNDERSTANDING

page 91

Here are the answers, with sample explanations given for the opinion statements:

    1. Fact. It can be proven.

    2. Opinion. Everybody has a different idea about what would be quick or slow.

    3. Opinion. Everybody has a different idea about how awkward something is to handle.

    4. Opinion. Everybody has a different idea about what makes up a long distance.

    5. Fact. It can be proven.

    6. Fact. It can be proven.

CHECK YOUR UNDERSTANDING

page 94

Here are some sample answers:

    1. Natural Bug Killer is a safe insecticide to use.

    2. The ingredients in Natural Bug Killer are completely safe for the soil.

    3. Toxins in Natural Bug Killer will break down very fast.

    4. Insects will die quickly.

    5. Making Natural Bug Killer solution is simple to do.

    6. Customers will get refunds back in a short time.

LESSON WRAP-UP

page 95

Here are some sample answers:

    1. Identifying facts and opinions can improve my reading because it helps me understand ads better.

    2. I was an office clerk. Once, I received an office memo about the office kitchen. It talked about how some people were not using the microwave properly. It was important that I knew which details were facts and which were opinions. That's because the facts were things that I had to do and follow. The opinions were not.

Lesson 12: Caring for Plants and Lawns

CHECK YOUR UNDERSTANDING

page 99

    1. c

    2. a

    3. c

    4. b

    5. d

CHECK YOUR UNDERSTANDING

page 102

Here are some sample answers:

    1. One difference between natural and regular lawn care is the type of fertilizers that are used. With natural lawn care, organic fertilizers are used. Non-organic fertilizers are used with regular lawn care.

    2. Organic fertilizers are probably better for the soil. That's because organic fertilizers break down slowly into nutrients that the soil needs.

    3. Grass clippings can be messy on the lawn if they're in big, dry clumps. But it doesn't have to be messy. If you mow the lawn so that only a small amount of it is cut, the grass clippings will just fall into the lawn. You won't be able to see them. They are also a natural fertilizer.

4. If it's true that non-organic fertilizers are not bad for the soil, humans and animals, and even the lawn, then everyone should change to natural lawn care.

5. I would want to care for the lawn in the easiest and cheapest way. And that seems to be the natural way. I wouldn't have to rake the grass clippings after I mow the lawn. Also, I wouldn't have to water as much.

LESSON WRAP-UP
page 103
Here are some sample answers:

1. Drawing conclusions can help me put my reading to good use because I can use information to come to new understandings when solving a problem.

2. I was a warehouse worker. I had to read some papers and choose an insurance plan that the company paid for. Drawing conclusions helped me figure out what plan was the best for me.

UNIT 4 REVIEW
page 104

1. Accept answers in any order:
   a. One detail is a common problem that might happen to a machine.
   b. One detail is one or more possible causes for the problem.

2. A fact is a detail that is true or can be proven as true. An opinion is an author's feeling, belief, or thought that may or may not be true.

3. Accept any of these answers for a. and b.

One reason is that I would need to make a judgment about that writing. Or: One reason is that I would need to give an opinion about that writing. Or: One reason is that I would need to make a decision based on the details in that writing.

4. Accept all reasonable answers. For example: I would be interested in being a private gardener. I like working outside, and I like growing plants and taking care of them. I also like the idea of being my own boss. Having strong reading skills would be important for this job. I would have to handle a lot of paperwork as a boss. And I would need to read materials to keep up on new and better ways of gardening.